Machine Knitting

THE TECHNIQUE OF PATTERN CARD DESIGN

Machine Knitting

THE TECHNIQUE OF PATTERN CARD DESIGN

DENISE MUSK

B. T. Batsford Ltd

For Emma and Thomas, my grandchildren

Typeset by Servis Filmsetting Ltd, Manchester and printed in Great Britain by
Butler & Tanner Ltd
Frome, Somerset

Published by B T Batsford Ltd
4 Fitzhardinge Street, London W1H 0AH

A catalogue record for this book is available from the British Library

ISBN 0 7134 6439 9

My thanks to Michael Brooks of Yeoman Yarns, and Ian and Jackie Mitchell of Worth Knitting for supplying the yarn for sampling. Thanks are also due to David Lowdell the photographer. A special thank you to Jean Smith who did the sample of handknitting, and to my City and Guilds' students who helped to iron out some of the problems which occurred whilst preparing the manuscript – especially Barbara Wade who simplified the problem of marking transfer lace.

Note   At the time of going to press Silver Reed knitting machines were marketed under the name of Knitmaster UK.

DM 1992

CONTENTS

CONTENTS

INTRODUCTION

Learning how to create patterncards for a knitting machine opens up a whole new world to the machine knitter. No longer is one tied to stitch patterns which are presented in books and magazines. Each garment produced can differ from the previous one because the patterncard has been altered in some way to add a new dimension to the garment.

Understanding the pattern system which is being used and how the patterncards fit into that system is vital to successful patterncard designing. In the following chapters the basic stitch settings will be looked at to establish the type of patterncard required for each stitch, to observe the effect of the selected stitch on the fabric structure and to analyse how to create patterncards for the chosen setting.

When the basic technique of patterncard design has been mastered, chapter 8 explains how to extend the use of some of the patterncards designed in earlier chapters. A totally different effect can be created if a patterncard is used in conjunction with a yarn or a cam change, extra rows are introduced to the patterncard or the stitch settings are combined in various ways.

Learning to manipulate the patterncards in this way gives the knitter mastery over the machine and can lead to some exciting discoveries.

Note The word patterncard is being used throughout the book instead of punchcard, in order to indicate that the same methods can be used to design punchcards, mylar sheets and computer programs. Where the method of design differs it is specified in the text.

1 THE EVOLUTION OF THE PUNCHCARD

The punchcard has been around since the early eighteen hundreds. Joseph Marie Jacquard developed it for use on weaving looms. It was adopted later in the century by the knitwear manufacturers and remained in use in the industrial sector until the new breed of home knitting machines was developed in the middle of the twentieth century.

The modern domestic punchcard knitting machine evolved from the push button machines with an eight stitch pattern base, which needed a lever to select the pattern, through to the familiar twenty four stitch punchcard machine. Technology has advanced even further and it is now possible to enter a pattern into a computer, connect it to the knitting machine, and knit it. New technology enables the knitter to control every one of the two hundred needles individually.

Eight stitch pattern base

The eight stitch pattern base is used on the semi automatic machines. (The Brother 710 is an update of these early machines.) Buttons are used to select the pattern sequence which is printed on a chart. The needles are placed in the patterning position by pulling a lever on the machine. This lever is operated every pattern row and the buttons must be changed manually each time the pattern alters which makes patterning rather tedious.

Twelve stitch pattern base

The twelve stitch pattern base is used by the Jones/Brother 800 and the Toyota 747 knitting machines.

The Jones 800 is a semi-automatic punchcard machine. The pattern selection is by punchcard but the needle selection is made by operating a lever. This method of selection speeds up pattern knitting considerably and was a decided advance on button pushing. Manual intervention is needed on the more complicated patterns and, as with the eight stitch discipline, a chart is used to give these instructions (figure 1). These charts can be converted for punchcard use. The *Cassette Pattern Book* which comes with the machine is a very rich source of design ideas, particularly for lace.

The Toyota 747 also uses a punchcard in conjunction with a lever but in addition there are buttons. The use of both punchcard and buttons produces a wide variety of patterns which can be random or regular depending on the requirements of the operator.

Whilst these machines were in use a quiet revolution was beginning. The introduction by Knitmaster of their twenty four stitch fully automatic punchcard machine, the 321, was the turning point for machine knitting. With automatic punchcard knitting over twenty four stitches, the twelve stitch base appeared very restricting. It was not until the patterning chunky machines were introduced that the twelve stitch punchcard re-appeared. This time the patterning was fully automatic. The Knitmaster 155 uses the same size punchcard base as the twenty four stitch standard gauge machines but it uses only every alternate column. A twenty four stitch punchcard with double width marking can be used as it is on the 155 (figure 2). The pattern is twelve stitches wide instead of twenty four stitches.

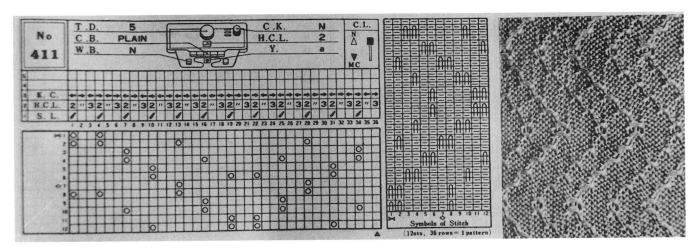

1 Chart 411 from *Cassette Book. Courtesy Brother*

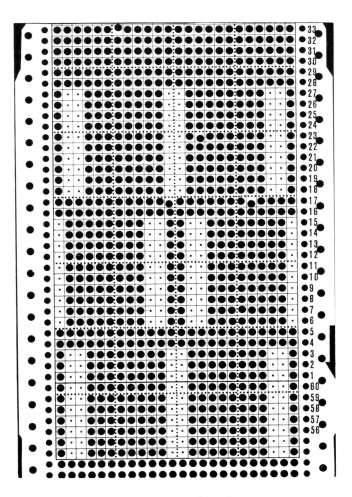

2 A double width marked punchcard

Twenty four stitch pattern base

The twenty four stitch pattern base is used by the standard gauge punchcard machines. Each manufacturer uses a different system to select the needles but all of them are fully automatic.

The Brother and Toyota machines pre-select the needles making the pattern row fully visible (figure 3).

Knitmaster machines select the pattern using the pattern drums at the back of the carriage. The needles stay in normal working position after the pattern has been selected. However, as the carriage is moved across the needlebed the pattern can be seen on the sinker plate assembly. Each movement of the carriage selects, knits, patterns and returns the needles to normal working position. The row which is to be knitted can be seen by placing the stop knob to the forward position. The levers which remain in the forward position when a punchcard is in place are the blank sections of the card (figure 4).

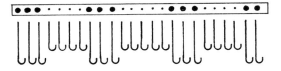

3 Diagram of pre-selected needles

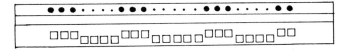

4 Diagram of Knitmaster pattern panel

Thirty stitch pattern base

The thirty stitch pattern base is used for the Knitmaster Fine Knitter which works and patterns in exactly the same way as the other Knitmaster punchcard machines.

Forty stitch pattern base

The forty stitch pattern base is used for the Passap and Pfaff machines. Pattern selection on these European machines is by a pusher system in combination with arrow keys (figure 5). The pattern is selected by the cardreader which can be placed anywhere on the bottom rail. By passing the deco (pattern selector), set to 'O', across the cardreader the relevant pushers are selected. When the deco is attached to the lock, and set to either 2 or 4, the patterning is automatic. In some patterns the left arrow key is depressed to reverse the pusher arrangement already in use. The needles always return to normal working position whilst the pushers indicate the next pattern row (figure 5).

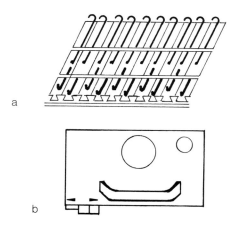

5 Section of Passap/Duomatic needlebed
  (a) Position of needles and pushers
  (b) Position of arrow keys with the left one depressed

Sixty stitch pattern base

The sixty stitch pattern base is used by the early electronic machines. These knitting machines are more versatile than those previously mentioned.

The user can determine how many stitches are required for each pattern, any number from one to sixty. It is possible to use the double width and mirror image facilities to produce a two hundred and forty stitch width pattern but with only two hundred needles available it is not feasible.

Two hundred stitch pattern base

It is now possible to control each needle individually either by using a number of patterncards or by using a computer attachment. The design possibilities are infinite. It is preferable that the operator has a basic knowledge of patterncards before embarking on a large design. There are many pitfalls for those without sufficient knowledge to foresee the problems. However, the prospect of a two hundred needle design is a challenge.

Despite the availability of two hundred stitch wide pattern bases the twenty four stitch pattern width has become a standard for machine knitting. Many patterns end up being twenty four stitches wide even when more stitches are available. The pattern repeats can be based on two, three, four, six, eight, twelve and twenty four stitches. These factors occur again and again in the stitch bases of the other machines; see table in figure 6.

Pattern width	Stitch base			
	12	24	30	40
2	√	√	√	√
3	√	√	√	
4	√	√		√
5			√	√
6	√	√	√	
8		√		√
10			√	√
12	√	√		
15			√	
20				√
24		√		
30			√	
40				√

6 Chart of stitch bases

The position of the patterncard on the needlebed

1 Japanese punchcard machines

The position of the punchcard on the needlebed is predetermined on the punchcard machines with twelve, twenty four and thirty stitch bases. The pattern panel and needle strip on Knitmaster machines are marked to indicate the relevant positions. Brother mark the punchcards and the needle strip (figures 7a and 7b).

2 European punchcard machines

The Passap/Pfaff machines with their forty stitch base and external patterning can have the cardreader placed anywhere on the needlebed. This is a useful addition to the machine facilities. However, it is important to note exactly where the cardreader is placed on the needlebed, as, if the cardreader is to be moved to a new position during the knitting it must be moved within the forty stitch discipline otherwise the pattern will be spoilt.

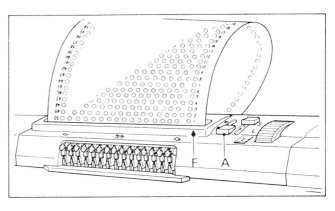

A = Stop knob
F = First row

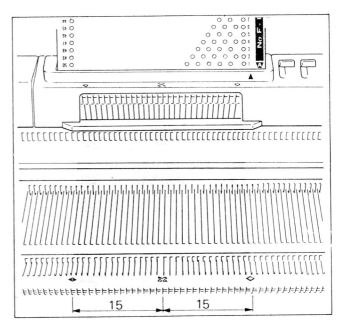

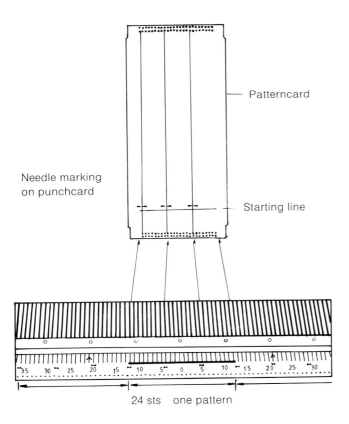

Patterncard

Needle marking
on punchcard

Starting line

24 sts   one pattern

7a Markings for Brother punchcards and needle strip

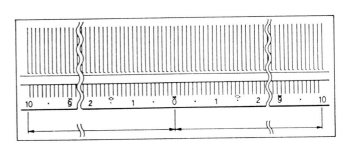

7b Markings for Knitmaster fine knitter and pattern panel. *Courtesy Knitmaster*

3 Japanese electronic machines

a Brother electronic machines are more flexible than the standard punchcard machines. The pattern can be placed anywhere on the needlebed when the single motif pattern selector (A) is used. There are no restrictions on the stitch width of the pattern and, as the patterning is internal the pattern centre should not need shifting unless it is to alternate the design.

b When using the allover pattern selector (B), with an even number of stitches to the pattern, the machine automatically places an even number on both sides of the centre (figure 8a).

c When using the allover pattern selector (B) with an odd number of stitches to the pattern the machine always centres on G1. Therefore there is one more stitch pattern on the right of the needlebed than there is on the left (figure 8b). On the Brother and 950i, using the 999 mode, the first needle position of an allover pattern can be altered; see page 33 of the manual for full details.

d The Knitmaster electronics (500 and 560) use the needle one cam (N1C) to determine where on the needlebed the pattern is to begin. As with the other electronics there are no restrictions on the pattern width. Point cams are used on the rear of the needlebed over the desired width of the pattern.

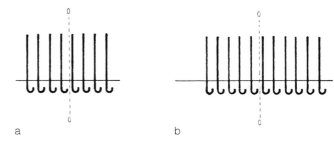

a　　　　　　　　　　　　　　b

8　Centring the patterncard on the Brother Electronic
(a)　Even numbered patterns
(b)　Odd numbered patterns

Patterncard markings

The Brother Pattern Programming Device has been used to produce most of the patterncards. In *Stitch World*, the book issued with the 950 and 950i machines, the patterns are presented with the same markings as conventional punchcards to simplify the knitting instruction, but only one pattern repeat is shown. When transferring the print-outs to a punchcard remember to repeat the design across the whole width of the punchcard and over at least thirty six rows to enable the card to rotate.

Using the patterncards

Follow the machine manual for any patterncard print-out which does not have knitting instructions.

2 FAIR ISLE

Fabric definition

Fair Isle knitting is a two-colour, double-thickness fabric. The face side has a smooth, coloured surface. The reverse side has strands of yarn which pass from one block of colour to another.

Fabric comparison

The Fair Isle setting narrows and elongates a fabric. There are more stitches and fewer rows to each centimetre than in stocking stitch.

Knitting method

The two colours are knitted simultaneously to produce a design which is the same as the reverse side of the patterncard.

1 The Fair Isle setting on the machine allows two colours to be knitted in a row at the same time. The main colour is in feeder A (Brother), feeder 1 (Knitmaster). The contrast colour is in feeder B (Brother), feeder 2 (Knitmaster).

2 The blank areas of the card knit the main colour. The punched areas of the card knit the contrast colour.

3 On a machine which pre-selects the needles it is possible to see how the machine interprets the punchcards.
　　a The needles served by the blank areas of the card remain in normal working position (WP).

b The needles served by the punched areas of the card are placed in upper working position (UWP).

By definition
○ The needles which remain in WP will knit the yarn in the feeder nearest to the gate pegs, i.e. the main yarn in feeder A
○ The needles which are in UWP will knit the yarn in the feeder furthest away from the gatepegs, i.e. the contrast yarn in feeder B

The same method of patterning is used by machines which do not pre-select the needles but the needle selection is not easily visible. The selection is done by the pattern drums at the back of the carriage. The needles move forward if the relevant part of the card is punched but it is not as obvious as the pre-select method. Watch the movement of the needles as the carriage is moved across the needlebed. It is possible to see the punchcard pattern emerging. However, the needles are returned to normal working position after the row is complete.

Patterncard definition and marking

Fair Isle punchcards usually have a balance of punched and unpunched sections (figure 9). Fair Isle forms range from traditional to modern, abstract to pictorial (figures 9 to 16). Each type is produced by the same method – it is the cards which differ slightly depending on the type of design.

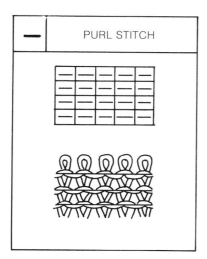

	PURL STITCH

9a (above) Purl symbol
9b (right) Typical Fair Isle punchcard
9c (below right) Needle selection   (i) Brother needle selection
                                    (ii) Knitmaster
9d (below) Knitted sample

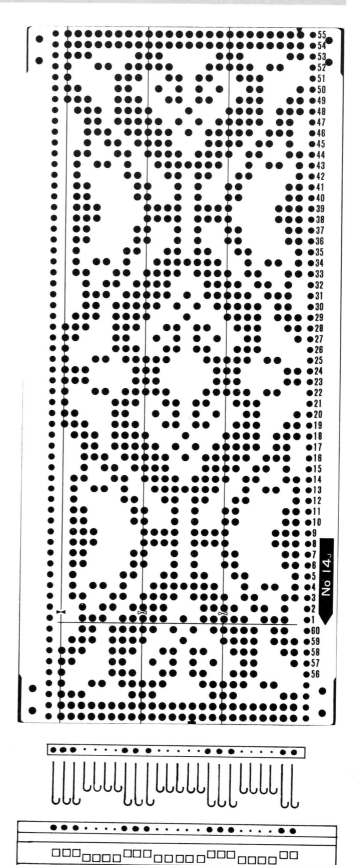

The patterncard marking is the same for all machines except when using the single-bed colour changers or a Toyota 787 machine.

The various categories of Fair Isle are listed below together with notes on the sort of pattern associated with each type, also guidelines on colour.

Traditional Fair Isle

The dominant patterns are separated by narrow borders (figure 10).

Any colour scheme can be used but if using a true Fair Isle border a frequent change of colour will look more authentic. Subtle colours are acceptable but insert a brighter colour to highlight certain aspects of the design.

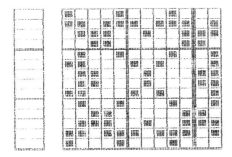

10a Traditional Fair Isle

10b Knitted sample

Motif Fair Isle

a Children's and fun motifs.
Simple designs with clear outlines (figure 11).
To emphasize the design use bold bright colours.

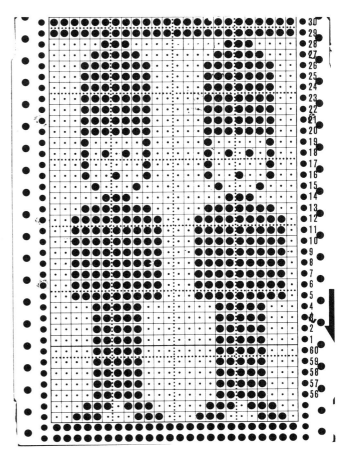

11a Children's motif punchcard

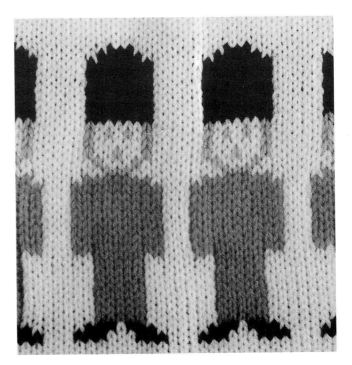

11b Knitted sample

b Single motifs.

Large designs with simple outlines.

To emphasize the design use bold bright colours (figure 12).

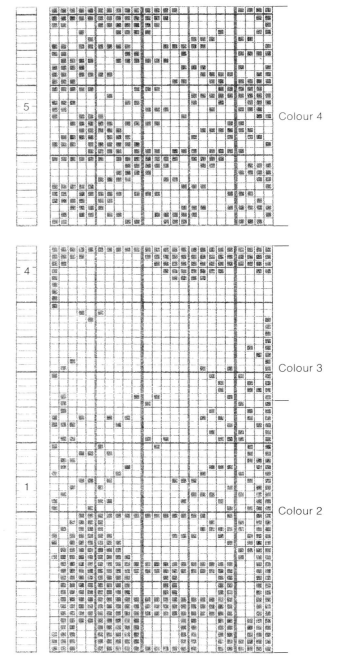

12 (above) Single motif – patterncard in figure 17

13a (right) Picture Fair Isle patterncard

Picture Fair Isle

There are two distinct types:

a Realistic natural patterns of which figure 13 is an example.

b Designs which are simple and childlike.

The realistic type of Picture Fair Isle requires colours as near to those in real life as possible. Use fine yarns which can be mixed to produce random colour effects throughout the knitting. The simpler type of picture requires a less subtle, more direct colour scheme.

Colour 4

Colour 3

Colour 2

Contrast yarn
Feeder 2

Background yarn
Feeder 1

Yarn type and colour selection

Colour 1 Dun-coloured polyster and silk 4 ply

Colour 2 4 ply white wool. Must be wool to produce the correct colour

Colour 3 Heather colour for the hills 4 ply

Colour 4 Natural colour for the sky. Two ends 2/16's wool

After 5 rows using colour 4, change it to the main feeder

Colour 5 Aran for the clouds. Two ends 2/16's wool

13b Knitted sample

Allover Fair Isle

This refers to any pattern which repeats itself continuously over the whole fabric without any obvious beginning or end to the design (figure 14).

Any colour scheme can be used in this type of design. Many of the allover patterns look equally good in any number of colour combinations.

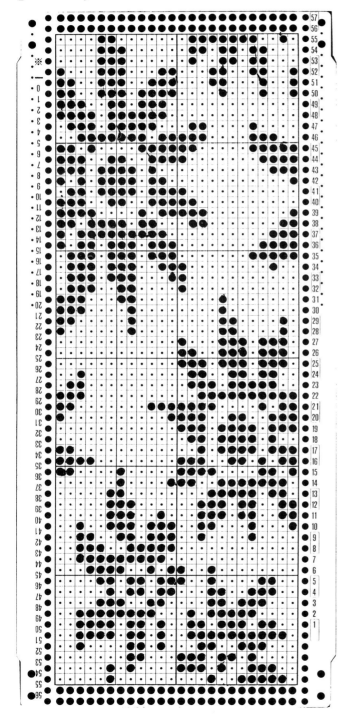

Embossed Fair Isle

This is any Fair Isle pattern with small floats and enclosed shapes (figure 15).

In this type of Fair Isle it is the contrast between the textures which is most important. As a general rule two tones of the same colour look very effective.

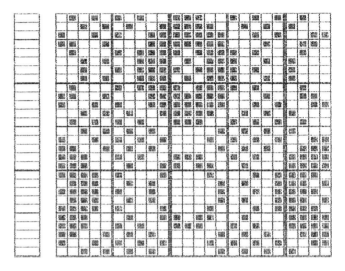

15a Embossed Fair Isle – Adapted Brother punchcard. *Courtesy Brother*

Yarn type

Colour 1 Background yarn – one end fine textured yarn plus one end 2/30's natural yarn
Colour 2 Contrast yarn – a toning smooth yarn

Geometric Fair Isle

This consists of simple geometric shapes. These shapes can be manipulated by the clever use of colour to produce designs which disguise the original pattern on the card.

Use bold, bright colours to emphasize the shapes, or subtle colours for a softer look.

14a Allover Fair Isle punchcard (left). *Courtesy Knitmaster*

14b Knitted sample

15b Knitted sample

Punch or thread lace

Punch or thread lace designs are usually allover patterns with large plain shapes outlined with lace-like areas knitted in fine yarn. The areas of fine yarn often use an every alternate needle arrangement which is two rows deep to emphasize the lace effect (figure 16).

Punch or thread lace is not an actual Fair Isle fabric although the Fair Isle cams are used to produce it. Two yarns are used, one of standard thickness the other much finer. Both are knitted simultaneously as with the Fair Isle setting but, where the card is marked, the single fine yarn is knitted on its own and, where the card is blank, both yarns are knitted together. Unlike Fair Isle there are not many floats. These are formed behind the punched areas of the card. The patterncards are mostly blank.

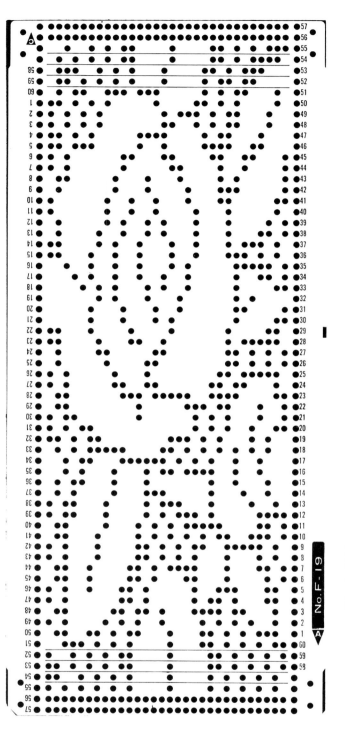

16a Punch lace punchcard for the fine knitter.
Courtesy Knitmaster

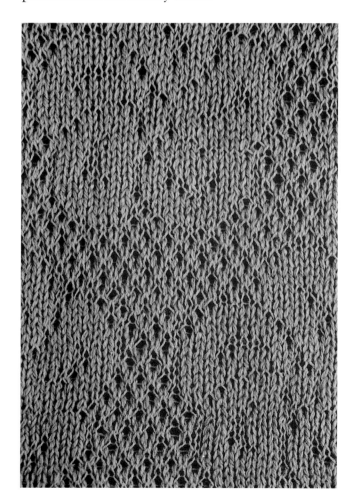

16b Knitted sample

A self-coloured fabric is very effective. Contrasting colours must be used with care as the design can be obscured if the wrong colours are used. The fine yarn tends to dominate the fabric as it is plated onto the surface.

Designing Fair Isle patterncards

The design methods used for all types of Fair Isle are very similar. The general guidelines below should help in the planning of basic Fair Isle patterncards. Where a specific type of Fair Isle design differs from the norm, the method is outlined in the section headed *Design methods for different types of Fair Isle* on page 22.

General guidelines for patterncard design

1 Stay within your pattern limits. There are ways of overcoming the pattern restriction which will be discussed later.

2 Keep the design simple. There are only a few stitches available and any fine detail may have to be eliminated.

3 Draw the design on proportional graph paper. The use of proportional graph paper for designing patterncards is now a well-established practice. The graph paper reproduces the proportions of a knitted stitch which is 1:1.3. Occasionally the desired shape is too large or too small for the pattern area available. To overcome this difficulty use a different sized grid. The proportions of the grid remain the same. A larger size grid will produce a smaller pattern. A smaller size grid will produce a larger pattern. Both will have an identical shape. More information is available on page 26, *Conversion from a thirty nine stitch pattern to a twenty four stitch pattern*, and in Kathleen Kinder's book *The Art of Motif Knitting and Twenty-four Stitch Design*.

The Brother mylar sheets for the electronic machines and Knitmaster punchcard packs come complete with graph paper of the correct proportion.

General guidelines for drafting a design

1 Decide on a subject.

2 Decide the type of Fair Isle. Check the list if unsure.

3 Draw an outline shape on plain paper or trace the shape from the design source (figure 17a).

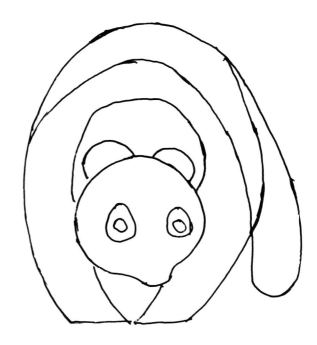

17a Outline of shape

4 Transfer the outline to proportional paper (figure 17b).

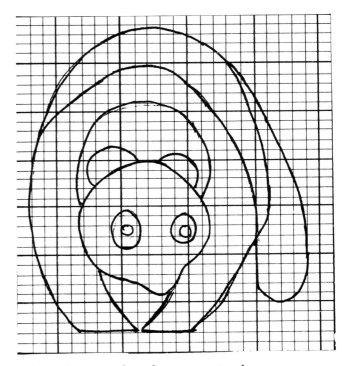

17b Outline transferred to proportional paper

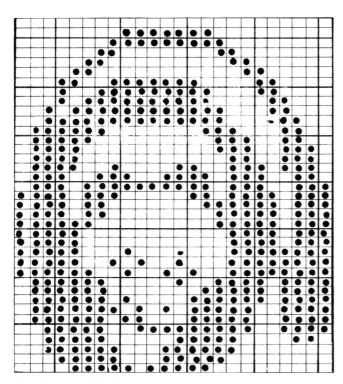

17c Outline filled in

17d Perfected punchcard

5 Fill in every rectangle which is completely enclosed by the outline (figure 17c).

6 Mark every rectangle which is three quarters enclosed by the outline.

7 If you have achieved a satisfactory design, although you may need to mark more rectangles, transfer the design to the patterncard and knit it to see how the design translates into knitting.

8 Make any necessary adjustments to the patterncard design. It may be necessary to fill in some of the squares which are only half enclosed in the pattern shape (figure 17d).

9 Re-knit if required. See figure 12 for the perfected design.

Design method for different types of Fair Isle

Traditional Fair Isle
Use the general guidelines.

Motif Fair Isle
Use the general guidelines taking care that the motif is in the correct proportion to the garment.

Picture Fair Isle
Use the general guidelines as a basis for design but avoid straight lines where possible. This is not difficult if the background and contrast yarns are changed on different rows.

When creating Picture Fair Isle it is sometimes useful to know how to increase the size of the pattern whilst staying within the twenty four stitch discipline. Study the photograph in figure 13. There are straight lines in this design as well as long floats. However, the design was the second in a series of picture hat and scarf sets. As each design developed new techniques were learned and these difficulties overcome. The main problem was to design a house and a tree with the correct proportions. To achieve this the tree was split in two with one half on the right and one half on the left of the patterncard (figure 13). This creates a pattern more than thirty stitches wide on a twenty four stitch punchcard. The design cannot be used as a single motif as the tree will be split in

half as it is on the patterncard. The second half of
the tree uses blank areas of the card not needed
in the main feature.

Allover Fair Isle

The types of Fair Isle described previously
produce repeating patterns but they do not
overlap, i.e. Traditional Fair Isle is mostly in
borders (figure 10), motifs are repeated but in
isolation (figure 12), Picture Fair Isle forms a
complete design vertically and repeats
horizontally (figure 13). The Basic Fair Isle
patterncards in common use produce a pattern
where the repeat is obvious and is an important
part of the design (figure 9). The allover repeat
patterns in this instance are meant to define the
more complicated designs where the repeat,
although present, is less obvious.

Sections of the design are arranged on the
patterncard in such a way as to disguise where the
design begins and ends both vertically and
horizontally. There are numerous ways of placing
the design on the patterncard depending on the
sort of repeat that is required.

To create an allover repeat pattern needs
careful planning. The main obstacle to be
overcome is the number of stitches which are
available for the pattern repeat. Most knitters
have only twenty four stitches to play with.

1 Sketch an outline of the desired pattern shapes
on plain paper (figure 18a).

2 Mark out a rectangle twenty four squares wide
and at least sixty squares deep on proportional
graph paper (figure 18b).

3 Transfer the outline of the main pattern shape
to the desired position. A cut out of the shape can
be moved around the marked rectangle to
determine the best position for the design. Its
position can be altered later if necessary.

4 Place the other elements of the design in their
relevant positions on the rectangle. Where a
shape overlaps the marked rectangle, mark it out
in full to see how the repeat will look and to check
whether there are enough blank spaces available
inside the pattern area to complete it (figure 18c).

Use in conjunction with the general guidelines.

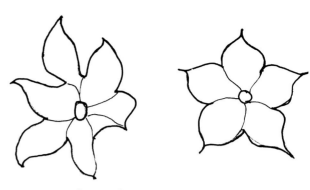

18a Original flower shape

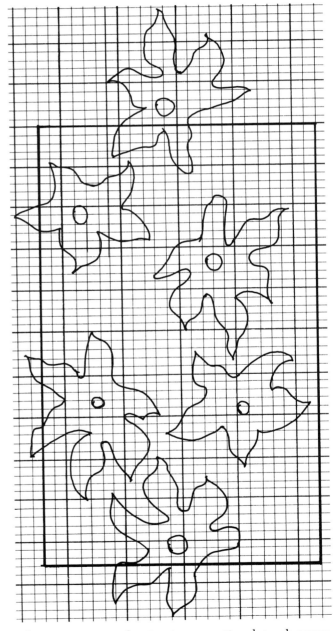

18b Design mapped out onto proportional graph paper

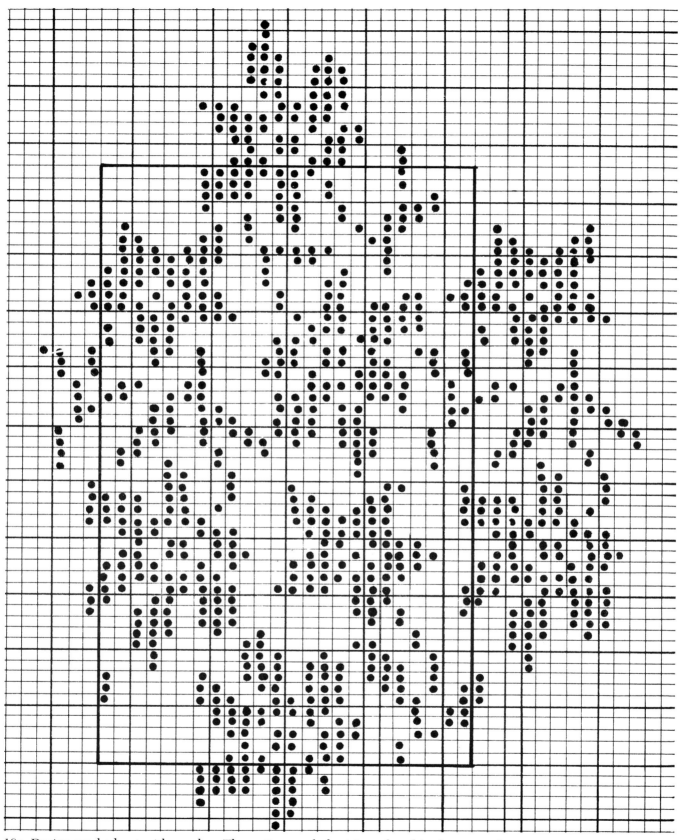

18c Design marked out with overlap. The patterncard chart is enclosed in the rectangle

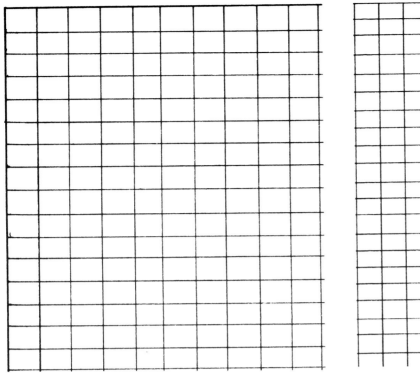

19a 12 stitch grid

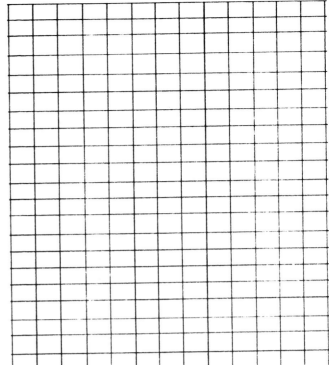

19b 15 stitch grid

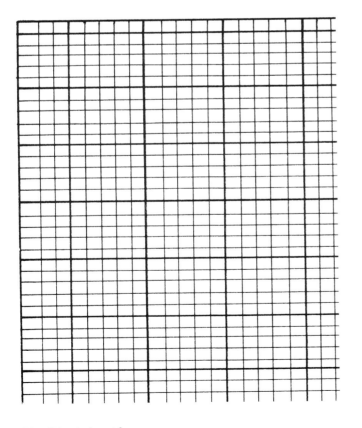

19c 24 stitch grid

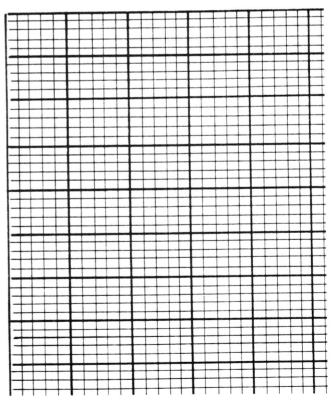

19d 30 stitch grid

Embossed Fair Isle
Use the design method for allover Fair Isle.

Punch or thread lace
Use the design method for allover Fair Isle. To produce a lace-like fabric the design should include areas with every alternate needle punching which are two rows deep (figure 16).

Geometric Fair Isle
Use the general guidelines. Patchwork templates are useful as outline shapes.

There seems to be some difficulty in increasing or decreasing the number of stitches in a pattern whilst retaining the same shape. Proportional graph paper is the key to solving this problem. Knitted stitches are not square. Their proportion is 1:1.3. Using graph paper with these proportions to design patterncards gives a true indication of how the design will look when knitted.

To obtain an identical shape which has a different number of stitches it is necessary to use different size grids in the **same** proportion. The grids in figures 19a to 19d illustrate the various sizes which can be used. They can be utilized to increase or decrease the size of a knitted motif or pattern without altering the original shape.

Altering the size of a design

The mylar sheet design in figure 20 can be reduced to a twenty four stitch pattern. There are some designs for the electronic machines which will be impossible to adapt, but knitters should not restrict themselves to the purchase of patterncard design books to those for their type of machine.

Conversion from a thirty nine stitch pattern to a twenty four stitch pattern

1 Trace the outline from the original design (figure 20a).

2 Transfer the design onto the twenty four stitch grid using carbon paper. Use *Densafilm*, a new plastic type carbon, if available. It will not smudge and gives a clearer outline than ordinary carbon paper (figure 20b).

3 Follow the general guidelines on page 21 for designing Fair Isle to create an outline of the pattern chart (figure 20c). Fill in the squares as before (figure 20d).

4 Transfer to the patterncard (figure 20e).

5 Knit the design (figure 20f).

The above instructions apply to all sizes of conversion.

20a Original mylar sheet design

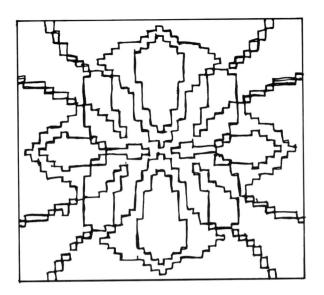

20b Tracing outline

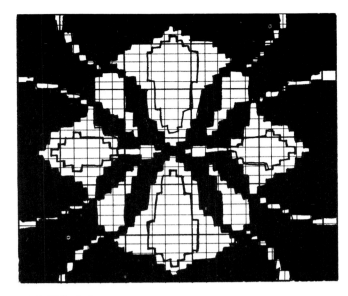

20d Filled shape

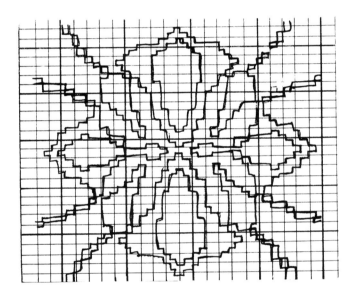

20c Outline transferred to proportional paper

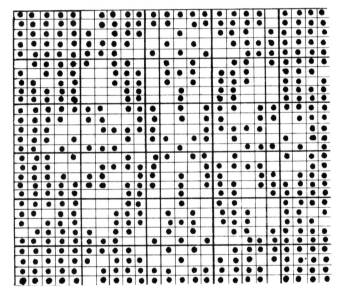

20e Patterncard chart

20f Sample of knitted fabric

3 SLIP STITCH

There are different types of slip stitch, for example basic, two-colour maze and mosaic, two-colour block slip, and petal slip stitch; each type is produced by knitting one colour at a time. It is the cards which differ depending on the example selected.

Fabric definition

Slip stitch knitting in its simplest form produces a slightly textured purlside fabric with strands of yarn across its surface. The knit (reverse) side of the fabric has an irregular stocking stitch appearance.

Fabric comparison

The slip setting narrows and shortens the fabric. There are more stitches and more rows to each centimetre than in stocking stitch.

Knitting method

1 The slip setting on the machine allows only one colour to be knitted at a time.

2 The blank areas of the card will slip. The punched areas of the card will knit.

3 On a machine which pre-selects the needles it is possible to see how the machine interprets the punchcard.

a The needles served by the punched areas of the card remain in normal working position (figure 21c).

b The needles served by the punched areas of the card are placed in upper working position (figure 21c).

4 The stitches on the needles in normal working position are bypassed by the carriage leaving a strand of yarn across the surface of the fabric.

5 The stitches on the needles in upper working position are knitted.

Punchcard definition and marking

Slip stitch patterncards have large areas of punching with the blank areas being no more than one or two squares across (figure 21a).

1 Punchcard machines must have the knitted areas punched.

2 Passap/Pfaff machines have the slip sections punched. The arrow key in conjunction with the deco card reverses the needle selection.

3 The mylar sheets for electronics can be marked either way. If the slip blocks are marked, the negative, number 6 button, is operated. In the *Stitch World* pattern book for the Brother 950 and 950i electronic machines the patterns are marked out in the conventional way, presumably because this eliminates the need to give extra knitting instructions.

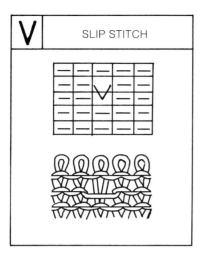

21a International symbol

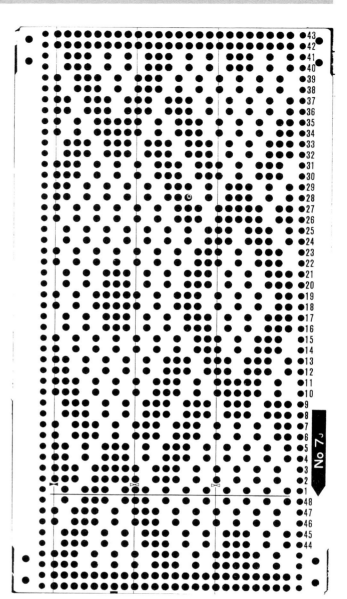

21b Slip stitch punchcard

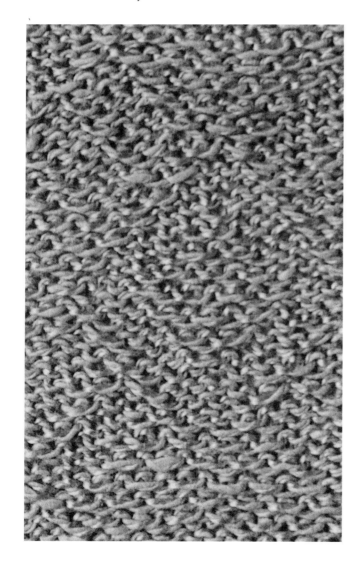

21d Knitted sample

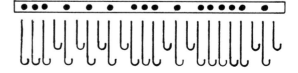

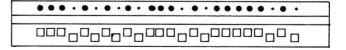

21c Needle selection

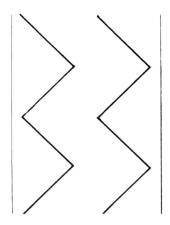

22a Outline of shape

Basic slip stitch

Basic slip stitch is not very exciting. The fabric is only slightly textured and most patterns are not very obvious (figure 21). There are numerous patterncards available for basic slip stitch. The slip sections can be allover or arranged in a geometric pattern across the fabric.

Designing basic slip stitch patterncards

1 Sketch out the shape required on plain paper (figure 22a).

2 Repeat the shape a number of times. Decide on the pattern filling and where to place it (figure 22b). It is obvious from the sketch in figure 22b that adjustments must be made to the original shape to accommodate the selected pattern filling and keep it correct.

3 Adjust the pattern filling as required (figure 22c).

4 Transfer the corrected pattern shape onto graph paper (figure 22d).

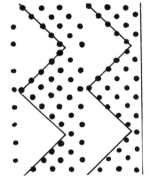

22b Pattern placement

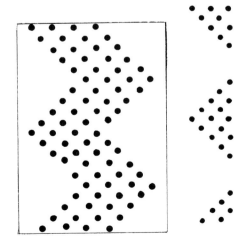

22c Adjusted outline

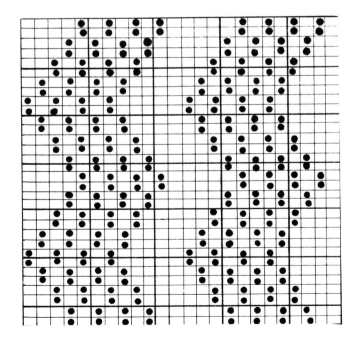

22d Transferred to proportional paper

5 Transfer the design to a patterncard reversing the markings (figure 22e).

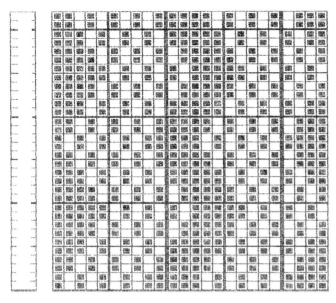

22e Patterncard

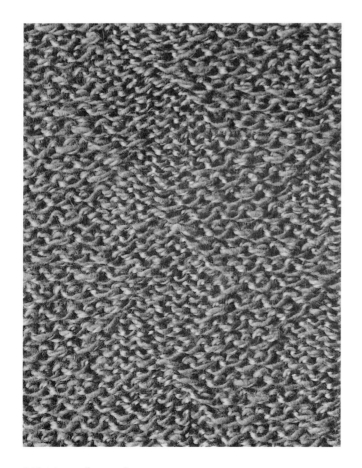

22f Knitted sample

Maze and mosaic slip stitch

Fabric definition

The knitside of the fabric looks like Fair Isle in that a two-colour pattern results but unlike Fair Isle the fabric is of almost single thickness with virtually no floats. The purlside of the fabric has stripes with short floats no more than two stitches wide (figure 23).

23a Two-colour slip stitch – knitside

23b Two-colour slip stitch – purlside

Knitting method

Knitting the basic slip stitch patterncards with a two-row, two-colour sequence produces a maze or mosaic design on the knitside of the fabric (figure 23a). To produce these patterns requires that the same needle selection is used for both rows knitted in colour 1. The needle selection then changes and remains the same whilst two rows of colour 2 are knitted. This process is repeated for the length required. The patterncards can be single or double marked. The knitting method is identical whichever marking is used. The machine must be set to elongate the single marked cards.

The pattern produced by knitting two rows of one colour and two rows of another does not resemble the punchcard in figure 21b. This is because the slip sections of the card hide the other colour on the purlside of the fabric.

To create a patterncard which produces a recognizable design is not possible when knitting two rows of one colour and two rows of a second colour in conjunction with the slip setting. Any basic slip card can be used with this method of knitting but the pattern it will form is not revealed until the knitting is complete (figure 23). However, if certain rules are followed it is possible to reproduce the pattern on graph paper without knitting it first.

Translating a slip patterncard onto graph paper to create a patternchart

Use the patterncard from figure 21b

1 Only one row of each double sequence is marked. To simplify the translation of the design, mark the patterncard into two row sequences. Number each one (figure 24a).

2 Using squared paper, mark the odd rows of the grid with the appropriate number (figure 24b).

3 On the odd numbered rows of the grid, mark the punched areas of the corresponding row on the patterncard (figure 24b).

4 On even numbered rows of the grid, mark the unpunched areas of the corresponding row on the patterncard (figure 24b).

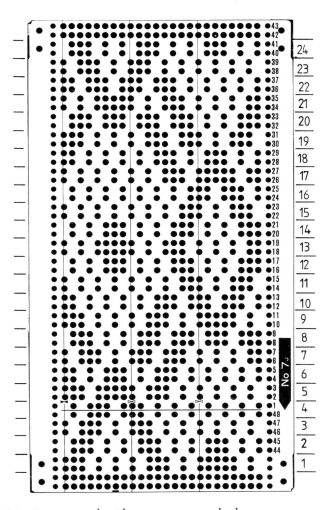

24a Patterncard with sequences marked

24b Marked grid

The pattern which is revealed is the one which would be produced using the two-colour knitting method described above (figure 23).

Single marked cards are transferred in exactly the same way but each row of the patterncard must be marked on the grid.

Rules for creating pattern charts for maze and mosaic knitting

Working on squared paper, mark all the odd numbered rows and stitches onto the grid.

1 On odd numbered rows any number of squares can be marked.

2 On odd numbered rows only one or two adjacent squares can be left blank.

3 On even numbered rows any number of squares can be left blank.

4 On even numbered rows only one or two adjacent squares can be marked.

5 Vertical lines must begin and end on odd numbered rows.

6 Vertical lines must be an odd number of rows.

7 The complete pattern must have an even number of rows.

Checking the patternchart

The international symbol for slip stitch, a 'V', illustrated at the beginning of the chapter, is used to check whether the design is correct. Each isolated mark/blank represents a slipped stitch.

1 Mark all the blanks on odd numbered rows with a 'V'.

2 Mark all the marked squares on even numbered rows with a 'V'.

If the pattern is correct each 'V' mark should be isolated, i.e. the squares both above and below the 'V' on the pattern chart should be identical. A slip mark on an odd row will have a blank square above and below it, a slip mark on an even row will have a marked square above and below it (figure 25).

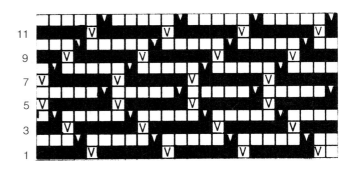

▼ Slip stitch on odd numbered rows
|V| Slip stitch on even numbered rows

25 Checking a maze design for mistakes

Designing maze and mosaic patterns

Maze patterns

1 Pencil in every odd numbered row across the appropriate pattern width (figure 26a).

2 Join the vertical lines at random (figure 26b).

3 Rub out those sections not required until a satisfactory design emerges (figure 26c).

4 The completed design with the pattern checked (figure 25).

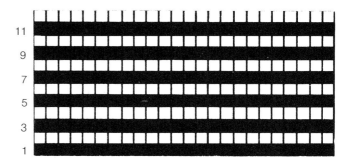

26a Mark grid and fill in odd numbered rows

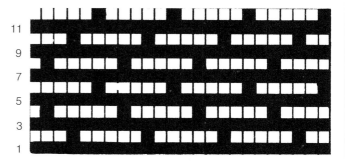

26b Join marked rows

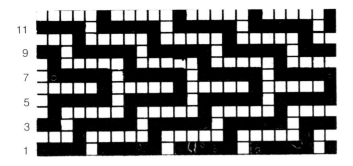

26c Rub out selected sections to reveal the design

Mosaic patterns

Follow the rules for maze patterns. In addition use a mosaic block which follows the rules, and build up a design from these (figures 27a–d). The block can be of any size as long as it follows the rules.

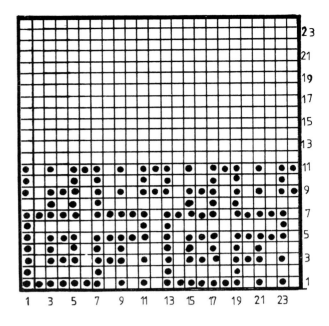

27e Design repeated over the width of the patterncard

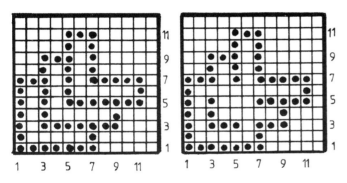

27a Mosaic blocks

27b Sections rubbed out

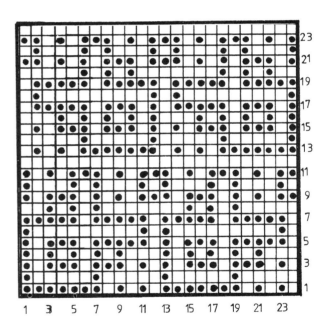

27f Completed design

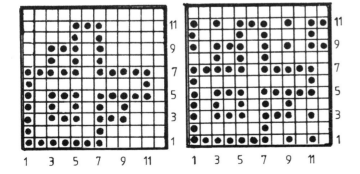

27c Sections added to keep the design correct

27d Perfected shape

Figure 28 illustrates the basic patterns used in mosaic knitting. Combinations of these markings are the basis of all mosaic designs.

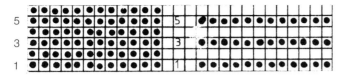

28a Total punching produces horizontal stripes

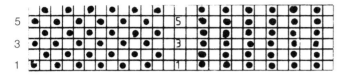

28b Every alternate square punched produces vertical stripes

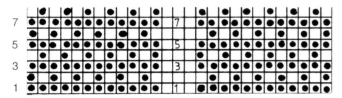

28c Alternating rows of total punching and every alternate needlepunching produces a checkerboard effect with colour 1 as the predominant colour

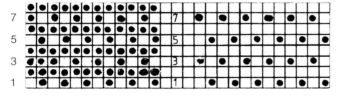

28d Reverse 28c marking to produce a checkerboard effect with colour 2 as the predominant colour

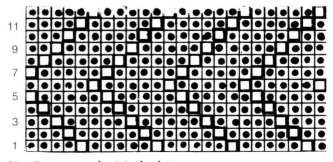

28e Mosaic block – can be of any size

Converting a pattern chart to a working chart

Method 1 (figure 29a)

a Number the odd rows on the empty grid.
b Mark all the 'V' symbols in the corresponding square on the working chart.

Add 1 row

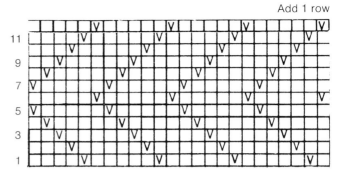

29a Method 1 – Mark 'V' symbols

Method 2 (figure 29b)

a Number the odd rows on the empty grid.
b On odd numbered rows mark the marked squares from the patternchart.
c On even numbered rows mark the blank squares on the patternchart.

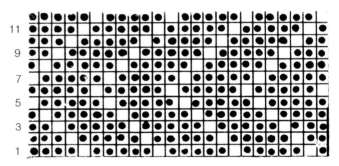

29b Method 2 – Mark as instructed

Converting the working chart to a patterncard

Method 1 (figure 29c)

a Outline every square marked with a 'V' symbol.
b Mark/punch all other squares.

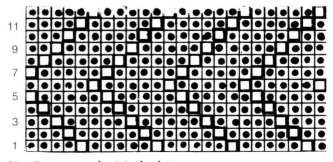

29c Patterncard – Method 1

Method 2 (figure 29d)
Transfer the working chart to the appropriate patterncard doubling the markings if desired.

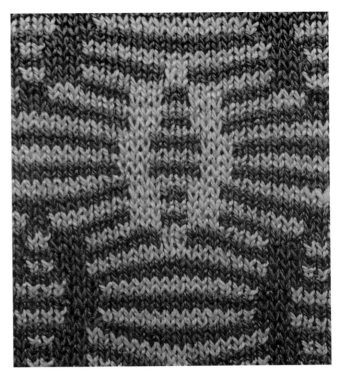

29d Patterncard – Method 2

Yarn
Any thickness up to 4 ply

Knitting instructions
1 Cast on required number of stitches
2 Set machine as appropriate
3 Knit in slip stitch throughout, changing yarn every 2 rows as indicated

30 Block slip

Designing patterncharts for block slip

1 Colour in every odd numbered row of the empty grid as in figure 26a.

2 Rub out the shape required in colour 2 (figure 31a).

Block slip stitch

Fabric definition

Block slip stitch produces a two-colour striped fabric with solid blocks of colour arranged in a predetermined pattern across the knitside of the fabric. The fabric is virtually of single thickness. Short floats which are no more than four stitches across occur behind the blocks of colour (figure 30).

This type of slip stitch uses the same method of knitting as maze and mosaic slip stitch but up to four adjacent stitches may be slipped. The fabric pattern features a striped background with solid shapes in both colours (figure 30). The colour of the solid shape is determined by the row on which it is begun, i.e. shapes which begin on odd numbered rows will be in colour 1; shapes which begin on even numbered rows will be in colour 2.

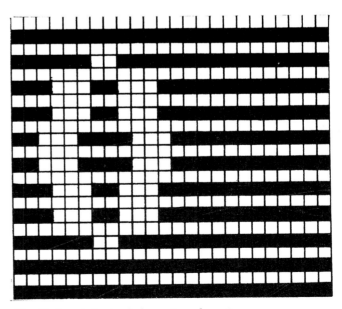

31a Rub out desired shape in colour 2

3 Mark in pencil the shape required in colour 1 (figure 31b).

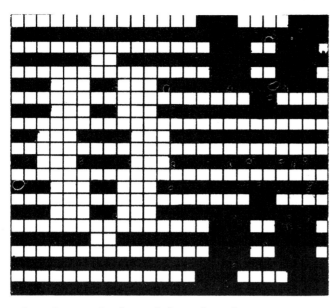

31b Colour in the desired shape for colour 1

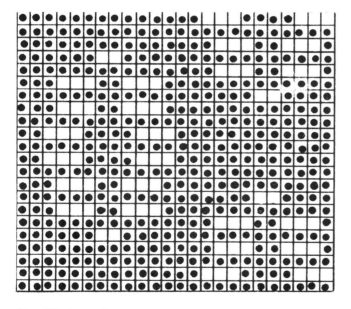

31c Working chart

Checklist

Use the same method of checking that the pattern is correct as used for maze and mosaic. Instead of single 'V' marks there will be groups along a row.

Translating a patternchart to a working chart

Follow the instructions for translating maze and mosaic designs to working charts using either method.

Converting the working chart to a patterncard

Follow the instructions for converting maze and mosaic working charts to patterncards (figure 31d).

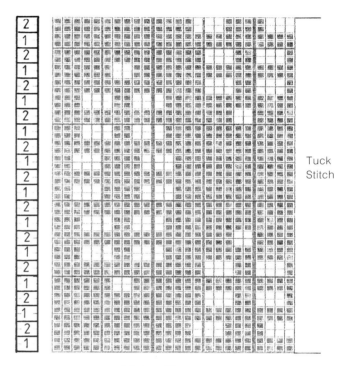

Tuck Stitch

24 sts   44 rows

31d Patterncard

Yarn type
Colours 1 and 2 Yarns of equal thickness

Knitting instructions
1 Cast on the required number of stitches
2 Set the machine and carriage as appropriate
3 Knit in tuck stitch, changing the yarn as indicated on the patterncard

Petal slip stitch

Fabric definition

Petal slip stitch produces a highly textured pattern on the knitside of the fabric. The surface pattern bears no apparent relationship to the patterncard with which it is knitted.

Designing petal slip stitch

Before designing petal slip stitch patterncards it is essential that the principles of the technique are understood. The pattern card in figure 32

incorporates a number of features which are the main characteristics of petal slip stitch. Figure 33a is a diagram of the patterncard in figure 32, knitside facing. To simplify the explanation each area of the card has been labelled in order to identify its function (figure 33b).

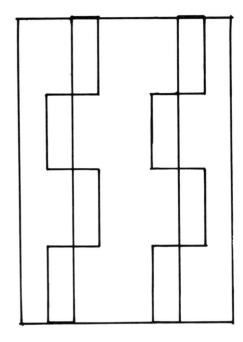

33a Diagram of patterncard in figure 32 (knitside)

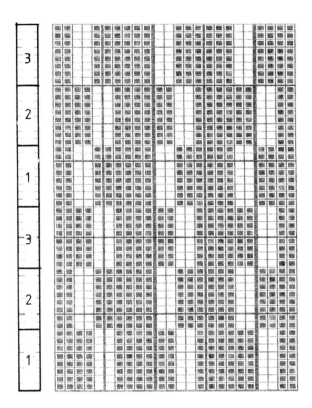

32 Patterncard for 'D' shaped slip stitch

Yarn type
Colours 1, 2, and 3 Yarns of equal thickness in either toning or contrasting colours

Knitting instructions
1 Cast on the required number of stitches
2 Set the machine to elongation and carriage as appropriate
3 Knit in slip stitch throughout changing the yarn as indicated

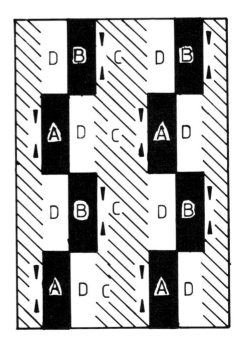

33b The various sections identified (knitside)

1 The slip blocks, A and B, are placed respectively to the left and right of a pivot line.

2 They are both two stitches wide and are placed two squares along the patterncard on a different level.

The placing of the blocks along a pivot line on different levels, and the knitting of sixteen rows in each section, causes the fabric to distort and produce unexpected patterns in the fabric. The two stitches wide slip blocks help to create the illusion of a fabric without floats.

Note Single stitch slip blocks can be used on occasion but they do not have the strength to hold the distorted fabric securely.

Explanation of figure 33b

1 The slip blocks on the left of the pivot line, marked A, will collect the knitting on the left of the block (figure 33b).

2 The slip blocks on the right of the pivot line, marked B, will collect the knitting on the right of the block (figure 33b).

3 The sections marked C, will knit every row (figure 33b).

4 The sections marked D, will knit on alternate blocks as the needle selection changes (figure 33b).

5 Figure 33d is colour coded to aid the explanation. When the patterncard is knitted the slip blocks A and B disappear completely from the plan (figure 33e).

6 The space created by the collection of knitting behind the slip blocks is filled in with the extra rows from section D which slide into the available space (figure 33f).

To check this statement knit each sixteen row section in a different colour. It will be seen that in figure 33e sections D and C on the left and C and

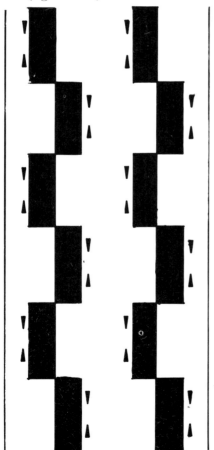

33c Arrows indicate where the knitting will collect on the purlside of the fabric

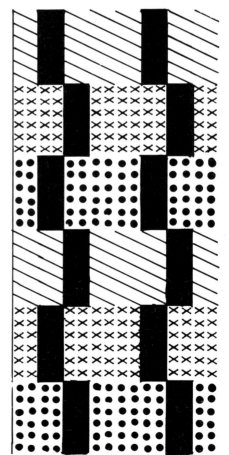

 Colour 1
Colour 2
Colour 3

33d Diagram of punchcard with colour key

33e The knitside of the fabric illustrating the collection of colours behind the slip bars

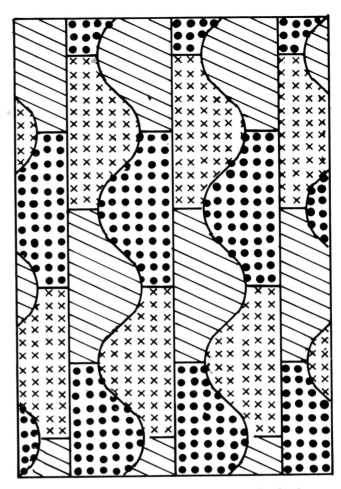

33f The knitside of the fabric illustrating the final distribution of the colour sections

D on the right of the line form a complete section. However, each part is manipulated in a different way by the patterncard.

Summary of characteristics

1 A slip block on the patterncard means that the knitting will gather behind these blocks (figure 33c).

2 Where two slip blocks are separated by a punched area of card the knitting from this section will spread into the area of the slip blocks as the knitting progresses (figure 33f).

3 Total slip stitch forms a pattern with a pointed outline (figure 35).

4 Slip stitch interrupted by stocking stitch forms a pattern with a rounded outline (figure 36).

5 Where the slip blocks are on a different level the knitting is dragged into other sections of the fabric (figure 35).

Note It is not possible to work single motifs using this technique as the sections which do not slip will only produce stripes. If single width motifs are desired then strips of the chosen pattern can be knitted and used as inserts in the knitted item.

Ruched Slip Stitch

Putting into practice what has already been explained should help in the pictorial development of these designs. Not every shape will fit into the discipline. However, if the desired shape is drawn, any sections which require a slip section on the pattern will be signified by a point (figure 34a). Mark the slip block onto each point of the drawing (figure 34b). The resulting diagram is a blueprint for a patterncard.

Note The actual knitting will not produce such definite angles but the outline shape will be similar to the plan.

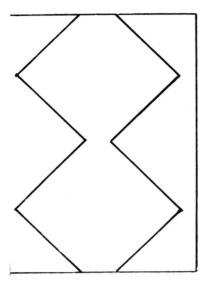

34a Diagram of desired ruched fabric

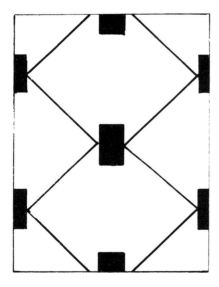

34b Slip blocks marked

Converting a slip pattern diagram to a patternchart

To produce an actual patterncard the design must be planned on graph paper before being transferred to a patterncard. Squared graph paper

is acceptable; each square represents one stitch and two rows of knitting.

1 Prepare the grid in the usual way over the desired number of stitches; a twenty four stitch wide pattern is ideal for a first attempt.

2 The slip blocks must have some stocking stitch rows between them to release the held stitches at intervals during the knitting. Try four rows on this pattern grid (eight rows of knitting).

3 Mark the slip blocks onto the grid; keep the eight row blocks (sixteen rows of knitting) used in the previous example for the initial design (figure 34c).

4 Place the second row of blocks the desired number of stitches away from the first and move down by half a block (figure 34c).

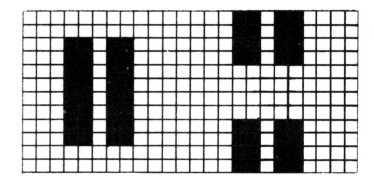

34c Slip blocks transferred to squared paper

A patterncard twelve rows deep and twenty four stitches wide has been developed. Mark it in reverse and double it. The potential of this one patterncard is wide indeed – it can be altered in numerous ways to produce a variety of effects, see chapter 8. The number of stitches between each block, the number of rows in each knitted section and whether the blocks are arranged in a half-drop pattern is entirely up to the individual.

Knitting method

1 The patterncard is knitted on elongation unless the card is double marked, see page 33.

2 The carriage is set to slip, and the knitting is worked without any cam changes for the desired length.

The fabric is a highly textured one with angled ruching (figure 34). It is interesting in a single colour but its potential is increased with the introduction of additional colours, see chapter 8.

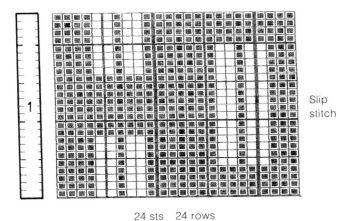

24 sts   24 rows

34d Patterncard with double marking

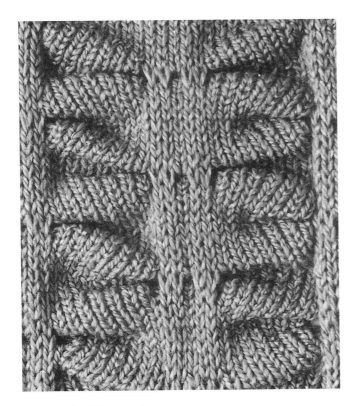

34e Ruched slip stitch

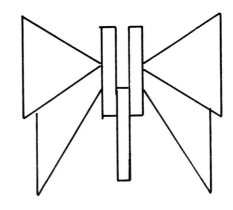

35a Butterfly outline shape

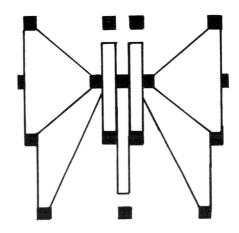

35b Butterfly diagram with slip blocks marked

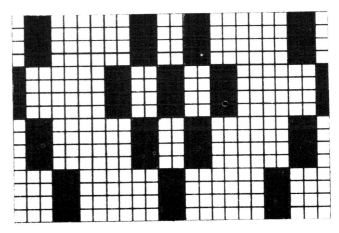

35c Slip blocks on grid

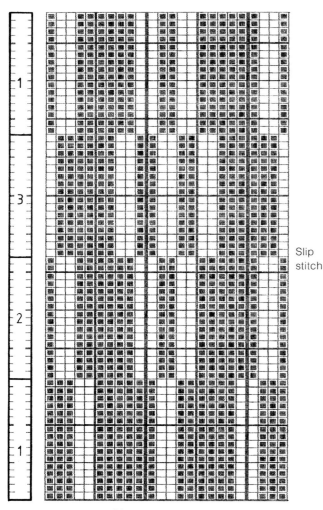

24 sts   64 rows

35d Patterncard with double marking

Yarn type
Colour 1 Background yarn – full 4 ply
Colour 2 Bottom wings – up to fine 4 ply
Colour 3 Top wings – same thickness as colour 2
The colours can be either contrasting or toning as desired

Knitting instructions
1 Cast on the required number of stitches
2 Set the machine and carriage as appropriate
3 Knit in slip stitch throughout changing the yarn as indicated

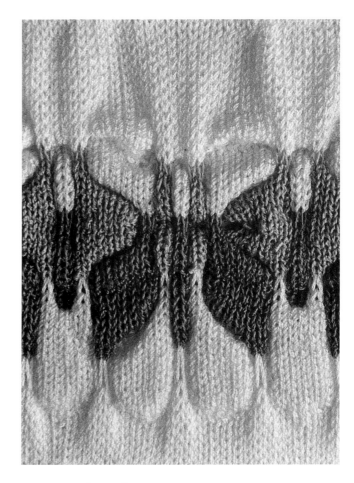

35e Knitted sample

Bubble stitch

Stocking stitch rows are needed to obtain a rounded feature in a slip fabric. The patterncard in figure 35 uses total slip stitch, i.e. there are no plain rows between the slip sections. The sketch in figure 36a suggests using circles in an allover pattern. These circles should form raised bubbles on the surface of the fabric. Because the circles are offset there is no need to introduce any extra rows between each of the vertical pattern blocks as the sections of the card which form the circles are not interrupted by slip blocks, i.e. they knit throughout the pattern.

Using the technique outlined above, and figure 34 as a guide, translate the shapes onto a graph paper chart to see how the patterncard will look (figure 36b).

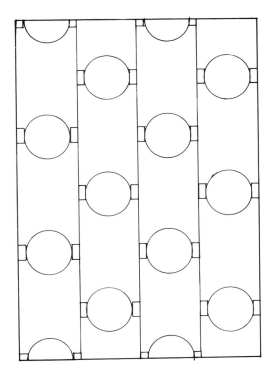

36a Initial idea

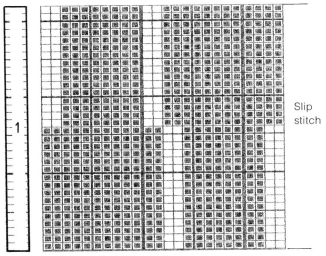

18 sts   28 rows

36b Patterncard: double marked

Yarn type
Any yarn up to 4 ply

Knitting instructions
1 Cast on the required number of stitches
2 Set the machine and carriage as appropriate
3 Knit in slip stitch throughout changing the yarn as
indicated

36c Knitted sample

Knitting method

Follow the knitting method given for the ruched
fabric, page 41.

The fabric produced by knitting the resultant
patterncard is unusual (figure 36c). In some ways
it is more successful than the ruched effect fabric
as it is lighter and softer but it is not perfect. The
sixteen rows used to form the pattern shape cause
too much fabric distortion between each of the
bubbles. Obviously the theory works but the
patterncard must be adapted to produce the best
fabric. By reducing the number of stitches and
rows in each pattern, and by adding two rows of
stocking stitch between each row of slip blocks, a
much more pleasing fabric which is lighter and
has more pattern definition than the original, is
produced (figure 36d). For more design ideas and
adaptations of the theme see chapter 8.

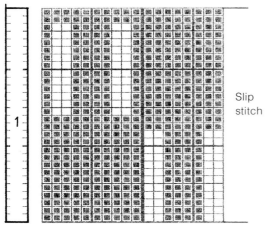

1

Slip
stitch

24 sts   32 rows

Checklist

1 The centre of each slip block will be the point where the extra rows will gather: mark this on the diagram (figure 33e).

2 Indicate, using arrows as in figure 33c, the direction of pull of the slip blocks.

For more patterncards using petal slip stitch see my book *Machine Knitting – The Technique of Slip Stitch.*

36d Perfected patterncard
  Knitting instructions as for 36b

36e Knitted sample of perfected patterncard

4 TUCK STITCH

Fabric definition

Tuck stitch produces a textured surface on the purlside of the fabric. The knitside of a single-colour tuck pattern has a textured surface but it is not as pronounced as the purlside. When colour is introduced either side of the fabric can be used. Each surface has a different finish. It is up to the individual to select the feature they prefer.

Fabric comparison

Because of the extra rows knitted to produce the texturing the fabric is more bulky than stocking stitch. The distortion of the fabric created by the extra rows forces the stitches outwards and compresses the rows. This results in fewer stitches and more rows to the centimetre compared with stocking stitch.

Punchcard definition

Punchcards for tuck knitting have more areas with holes punched than areas left blank. As a rule the blank (unpunched) areas consist of single blank squares across a row separated by areas of punching. The blank (unpunched) areas can be from 1 to 4 rows deep before the needle selection changes (figure 37b).

Knitting method

Only one colour can be knitted at a time unless the plating feeder is in use.

1 The blank areas of the card are not selected. The needles remain in working position (B) (figure 37c). When the tuck setting is in use these needles will come forward only far enough to collect a loop of yarn which will form the tuck stitches in the fabric (figure 37a).

2 The punched areas of the card are selected to upper working position (C for Knitmaster; D for Brother). These are the areas which will knit (figure 37c).

By definition, when the tuck buttons are depressed the needles which remain in working position will collect a loop of yarn which is held in the needle head until the punchcard selection dictates otherwise.

Note Tuck loops held in the needle hook are locked at the top of the stitch when released by the patterncard.

The needles which are in upper working position will knit the yarn in the main feeder.

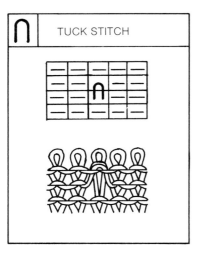

37a International symbol

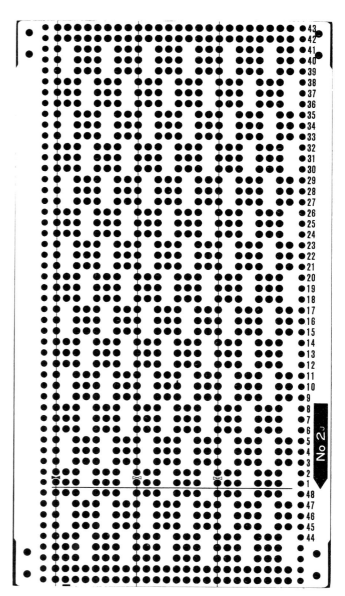

37b Typical tuck stitch punchcard. *Courtesy Brother*

37d Knitted sample

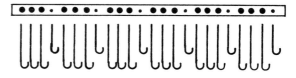

37c Needle selection and patterncard

Designing tuck stitch patterncards

The basic tuck stitch patterncards can be divided into two types.

a The small regular tuck patterns do not reproduce a replica of the patterncard. Depending on how the rectangular blocks of punching are arranged a number of different patterns can be produced (figures 37d and 38b).

2 sts   2 rows

38a Patterncard – card 1

b The larger geometric patterns which have chevrons, zigzags or diamond shapes at intervals over the card, reproduce these shapes exactly the same as the patterncard when they are knitted. Figure 39 uses the patterncard from figure 22 to illustrate the point. However, the larger shapes contain a small tuck pattern within their parameters making it essential that the small tuck patterns are fully understood before the larger patterns can be designed.

Tuck stitch cards can be difficult to create without this understanding. The following experiments will enable the individual to obtain this knowledge by observing and noting, on a checklist, the effects produced by the basic punchcards. In figure 40 a number of the most commonly used basic patterns are reproduced in

38b Knitted sample

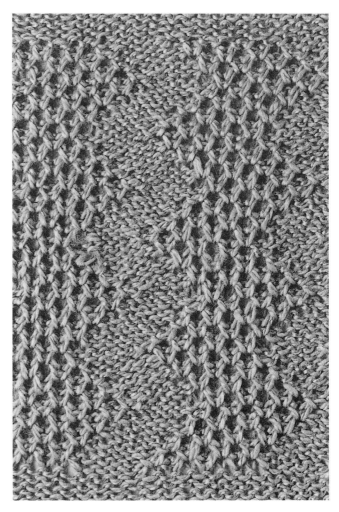

39 Tuck stitch version of figure 22

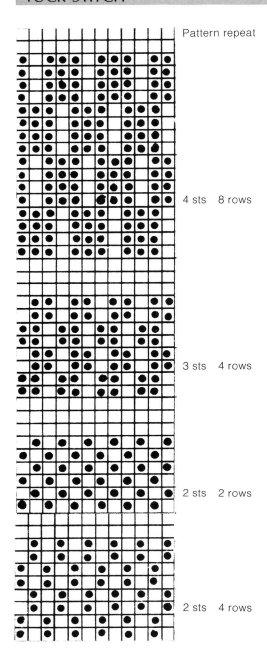

Pattern repeat

4 sts   8 rows

3 sts   4 rows

2 sts   2 rows

2 sts   4 rows

40 Charts of basic tuck stitch

chart form. The charts are marked over twelve stitches for punchcard machines. Remember to repeat the design across the punchcard and over sufficient rows to allow the punchcard to rotate. Duomatic owners must adjust the patterns to fit into their stitch discipline and mark the blank sections onto their punchcards. See the stitch chart on page 10.

Work through these cards using a 4-ply yarn, set the carriage to tuck and knit as follows:

1 as shown

2 with the machine set to elongation

Note If any difficulty is experienced with pushing the carriage **stop immediately**. There is no point in damaging the machine.

Example 1 will indicate the shape of the distortion produced by each basic pattern card.

Example 2 will produce the same fabric as previously but it will have a more distorted surface because of the increase in the number of knitted rows.

No difficulty should be encountered when knitting up to four rows of tuck. However, any pattern with more than four rows in the pattern could cause a muddle.

When knitting the 1 × 1 patterncard using the tuck setting a double-layered fabric is formed. The extra layer is created on the purlside of the knitting by the loops which are held in the needle hook on alternate needles and released every alternate row. These loops of yarn form a diamond shaped pattern on the surface of the fabric. The alternating stitches which are knitted on every row form the backing for the surface layer (figure 38).

When knitting the 1 × 1 patterncard using the tuck setting and elongation a thicker fabric is formed. Each needle hook holds two extra loops of yarn. The extra loop adds to the thickness of the fabric and causes it to distort (figure 41).

When designing tuck patterncards note must be taken of the properties of each basic tuck pattern. Tuck stitch widens and shortens a fabric.

1 A tuck fabric with one tuck loop and every alternate needle punching produces a bulky fabric (figure 38).

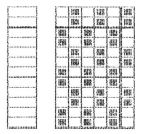

41a Patterncard – card 1 elongated

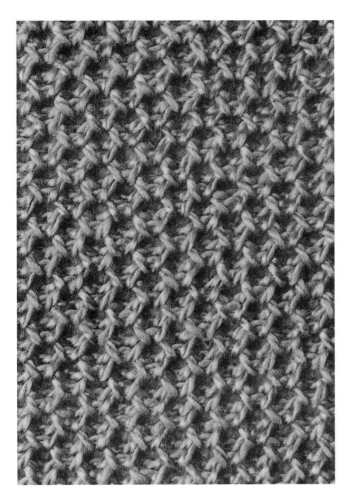

41b Knitted sample

2 A tuck fabric with two tuck loops and every alternate needle punching produces a fabric with more bulk than the previous fabric (figure 41).

3 A tuck fabric with four rows of tuck stitch and spaced out tuck sections produces a fabric which is longer than that produced by a patterncard with a 1 × 1 arrangement. It is lighter than either of the previous two fabrics (figure 37). It follows therefore that:

1 the thickness of a tuck fabric is determined by

  a the frequency of the tuck loops across the patterncard
  b the number of loops in each tuck.

2 a patterncard with every alternate square left blank will produce a wider fabric than a patterncard with every fourth square left blank: more tuck loops are held.

Designing large tuck patterns

1 Decide on an outline shape. Draw it on plain paper. Fill in the shape with the selected basic pattern (figure 42a).

2 The outline shape will have to be modified to accommodate the selected basic pattern (figure 42b).

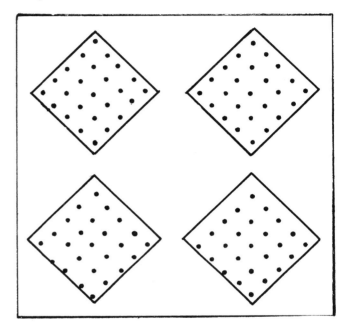

42a Outline of shape

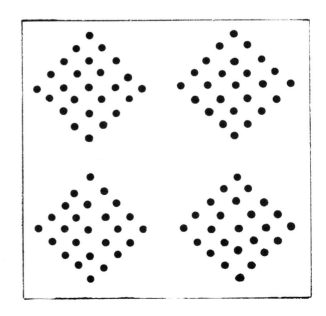

42b Adjusted diamond

3 Transfer to a patterncard reversing the markings (figure 42c).

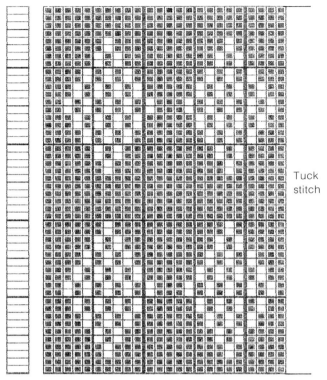

12 sts   24 rows

42c Patterncard

Variations

1 Any geometric shape will produce an interesting fabric. Varying the way that shape is filled will add more features to a design. There is no reason to restrict the filling to two rows of tuck. Combinations of two and four row patterns are most attractive.

2 Plan carefully where the geometric shapes are placed on the patterncard. If a number of squares are left clear of patterning for the length of the card another dimension is added to the fabric. But if too many areas have no patterning the fabric will have an untidy crumpled look.

3 Introduce plain stocking stitch rows to the patterncards between each change to the needle selection. This allows the introduction of colour, and different textures and thicknesses of yarn.

4 Introduce stocking stitch rows between each complete pattern section to produce isolated textured stripes across the fabric.

Planning the geometric shapes on paper is a useful exercise but in the end the design must be converted to a patterncard and knitted to see exactly how it works. In the case of the diamonds in figure 42, which are arranged in rows, the widest point of the shape occurs over just a few rows creating an unsightly ruching of the fabric. In theory if the diamonds are offset both vertically and horizontally then the widest point of the shape should be spread evenly over the fabric to create a much more pleasing effect. In practice more lumps are distributed at regular intervals over the fabric creating an interesting result which looks better on the knitside (figure 43b). The patterncard in figure 43 is an adaptation of figure 42 with elongation and alternating diamonds.

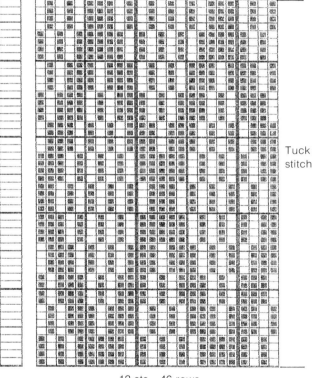

12 sts   46 rows

43a Patterncard for interlocking, alternating diamonds

Yarn type
Any yarn up to 3 ply thickness

Knitting instructions
1 Cast on required number of stitches
2 Set machine and carriage as appropriate
3 Knit in tuck stitch throughout

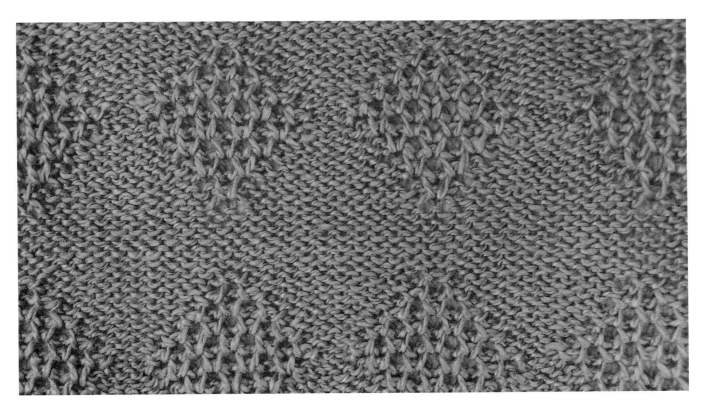

42d Knitted sample

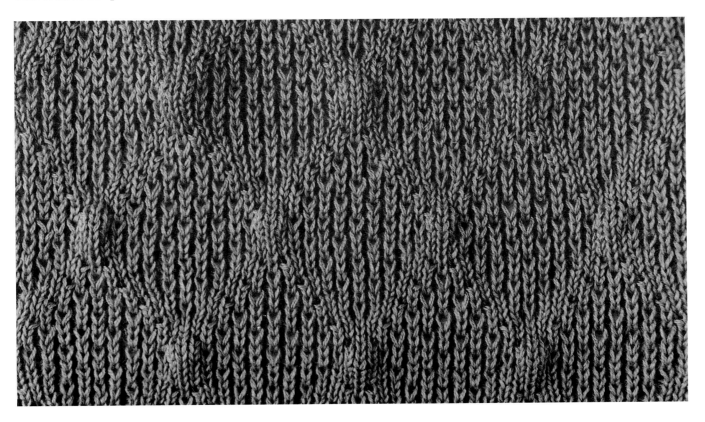

43b Knitted sample

Difficulties were encountered when knitting the patterncard in 4-ply yarn because of the number of rows which tuck and the frequency of the

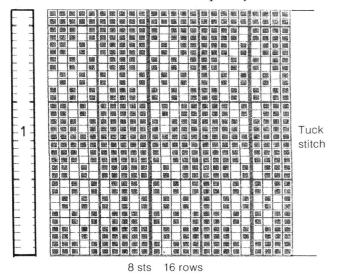

1

8 sts   16 rows

44a Patterncard for connecting diamonds

stitches which tuck across each row. A 3-ply yarn was used instead and no difficulties occurred.

To eliminate the ruching the diamonds can be increased in size so that they meet across the patterncard. This produces a fabric with an allover pattern which has alternating tuck and plain diamonds. When the fabric is released from the machine the stocking stitch sections have an undulating surface which may be of use in the development of other patterncards using tuck or any other stitch type. When the diamonds are reduced in size both horizontally and vertically the undulations in the fabric are reduced but it is not as interesting as the original (figure 44). However, the experiment has been recorded and a copy of the patterncards has been taken. The information will be filed away for future use. Anything which increases the understanding of a subject will be of use eventually.

Tuck
stitch

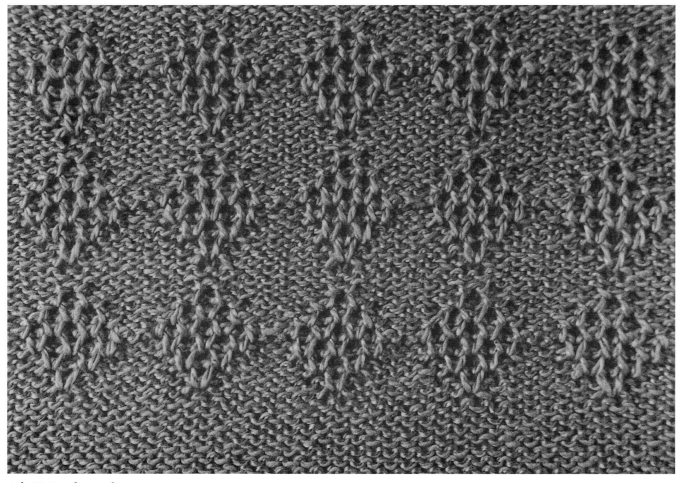

44b Knitted sample

New look tuck stitch

Next to Fair Isle tuck stitch is the most popular stitch setting used by machine knitters. Although there are many design possibilities with the basic cards tuck stitch has somehow taken on an old-fashioned look in comparison with the developments in slip stitch. The addition of colour adds another dimension as it allows the yarn to hide on the purlside of the fabric as in maze and mosaic knitting but, apart from this, tuck stitch conjures up a certain type of knitting often disparaged by those with no understanding of the craft. A pair of mittens given to my grandaughter had a most unusual raised design (figure 45). On close inspection the stitch proved to be tuck stitch. Updating tuck stitch had proved to be more difficult than anticipated. The experiments which had been carried out were not successful. The fabric in the mittens indicated where to direct the design development. A sketch of the fabric reveals an outline of the patterncard layout. It proved to be very similar to those for petal slip stitch (figure 46).

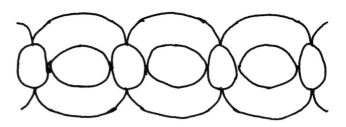

46 Sketch of new look tuck stitch

45 Mittens

The information given previously on designing petal slip stitch should enable the knitter to see where the tuck blocks must be placed. As stated previously, tuck loops hide behind the non-selected needles in a similar way to the strands of yarn in slip stitch. It follows therefore that sections of the drawing not included in the shapes will be the tuck areas of the patterncard. The design areas to be developed are the extra rows of stocking stitch between each change to the needle selection and the separation of each complete pattern to produce textured stripes. The observations already made at the beginning of the chapter indicate that the tuck stitch sections of patterncards are usually placed quite close together either over the whole fabric or contained in a geometric shape. Breaking up the tuck stitch into stripes and adding another yarn to the stocking stitch rows should help tuck stitch to advance in a similar way to slip stitch. The combination of the two variations with a planned spacing of the tuck sections reveals the design possibilities.

Designing the new look tuck patterncards

The new look tuck stitch patterncards are designed in a similar way to that used for slip stitch. The fabric gathers where the tucks occur but instead of the fabric collecting into the centre of the marked blocks, as in slip stitch, it will be lifted to the top of the block. The tuck stitch blocks will not be as deep as those for slip stitch as fewer rows are knitted but the same notation can be used to indicate the blank areas of the card.

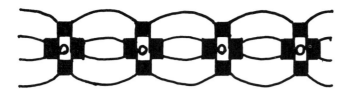

47a Diagram of fabric with tuck blocks marked

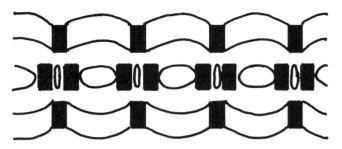

47b Spacing of diagram to indicate row sequences

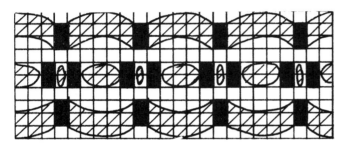

47c Square grid with different sections indicated. The grid indicates the number of stitches in each pattern repeat

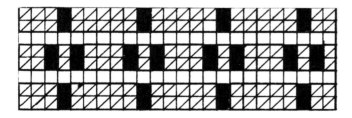

47d Layout of patterncard

Key

⬚ Tuckstitch

⬚ Stocking stitch with lycra

■ Tuck blocks

Preparing a working chart

1 Take a copy of the sketch in figure 46 and fill in the sections where the gathers occur (figure 47a). These blocks indicate where the tuck blocks will appear on the patterncard.

2 Shade in the areas enclosed by the pattern shapes. These areas will be knitted using the tuck setting (figure 47c).

3 The sections of the design remaining are the areas which will knit in stocking stitch.

4 Transfer the sketch with all its markings and shapes, onto a blank grid of squared paper, over the required number of squares.

The original pattern is six stitches wide. Each tuck block is four rows deep.

Note Tuck stitch compresses and widens a fabric. Each square on the grid represents one stitch and two rows of knitting (figure 47d).

5 Eliminate the curves in the pattern to reveal the layout of the patterncard (figure 47d).

Creating a new look tuck patterncard

1 The working chart represents one stitch and two rows for every square.

2 The shaded shapes and the blank areas will knit. Mark these areas onto a blank grid (figure 48a). Make sure that two rows are marked for every row on the squared grid.

3 Decide the number of rows required between the pattern bands. Mark these on the grid.

4 Transfer the finished design to the appropriate patterncard (figure 48b).

The patterncard in figure 48b using a six stitch, four row tuck pattern produces an interesting fabric but does not have the properties of the original (figure 45). The secret ingredient proved to be the use of lycra on the plain stocking stitch rows between the tuck sections. This addition pulls in the stocking stitch and raises the groups of stitches between the tuck sections above the level of the background fabric (figure 48d).

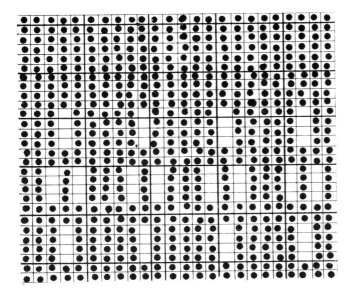

48a Chart of patterncard from figure 47

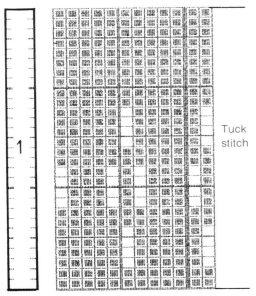

12 sts   28 rows

48b Patterncard for new look tuck

Yarn type
Any yarn up to 4 ply thickness

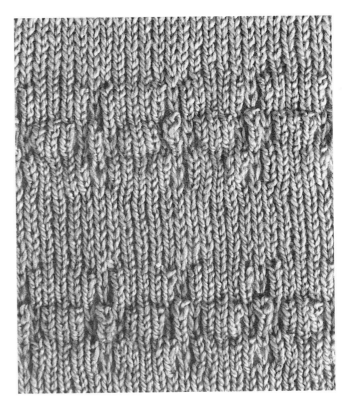

48c Original design

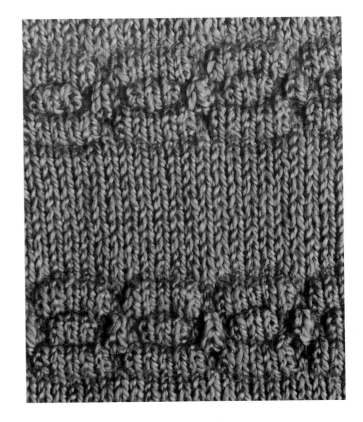

48d Perfected new look tuck stitch

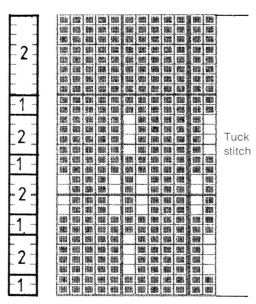

12 sts   28 rows

48e Patterncard

Yarn type
Colour 1 Main yarn plus lycra
Colour 2 Main yarn up to 4 ply thickness

Knitting instructions
1 Cast on the required number of stitches
2 Set the machine and carriage as appropriate
3 Knit in tuck stitch throughout changing the yarn as indicated

When the fabric in figure 48d is analyzed and compared with the patterncards the design possibilities become clear.

1 The four rows of tuck loops at each side of a single stitch in the centre of the design produce a raised ridge of knitting which looks similar to a bobble.

2 The same tuck loops form a raised section of fabric over the remaining three intervening needles.

3 The five stitch, four row sections at the top of the design form a downward curve.

4 The five stitch, four row sections at the bottom of the design form an upward curve.

5 These two curved sections outline the centre three stitches which are always knitted.

The shapes are much more pronounced than they would have been had four rows of slip stitch been used. This indicates that four row tuck blocks, distributed at less regular intervals than normal across a patterncard, can form a textured pattern on the knitside of the fabric. The pattern is not unlike petal slip stitch, but there are no floats whatsoever in the fabric.

The addition of lycra to the stocking stitch rows further emphasizes these features and compresses the design.

To develop the idea further take sections of the knitting, say sections 4 and 5 of the original patterncard, and draw the shapes offset from each other instead of directly above (figure 49). Develop the patterncards as described above.

When knitted, a cable effect results, not exactly as predicted in the diagram as the curve has been straightened out by the elimination of the centre

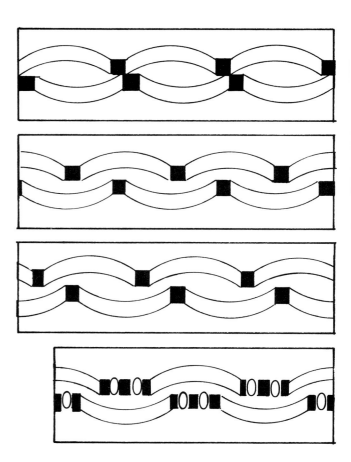

49a Cable effects

section of the design but, nevertheless, the effect will be a useful addition to the stock of new look tuck patterns. The design looks better when used sideways.

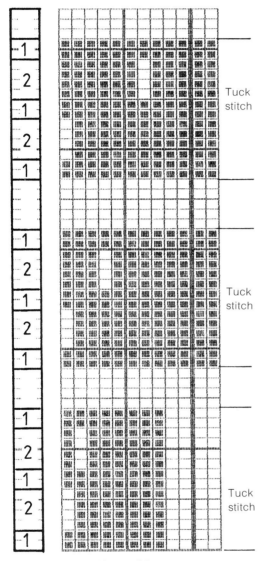

Tuck stitch

Tuck stitch

Tuck stitch

12 sts   54 rows

49b A selection of patterncards

Yarn type
Colour 1 Main yarn plus lycra
Colour 2 Main yarn any thickness up to 4 ply

Knitting instructions
1 Cast on the required number of stitches
2 Set the machine and carriage as appropriate
3 Knit in tuck stitch throughout changing the yarn as indicated

49c A selection of knitted cables

An interesting development is that the new effects have been produced using graphics. Sketching or outlining ideas on paper is something which is required by City and Guilds in their syllabus. Apart from designing Fair Isle, which is visual, a knowledge of how the stitch, fabric and patterncard relate is essential. Drawing simplifies design development and helps the individual to see how ideas are evolving without the need to knit too many samples.

In an attempt to create a textured cable effect the tuck blocks were placed in the centre of the outline cable block. The result in figure 50 would have been predicted if a diagram had been drawn. Figures 51a and b illustrate instantly exactly where the tuck blocks should have been placed. Convert the design to a patterncard following the instructions in figure 47 for creating new look tuck patterncards (figure 51).

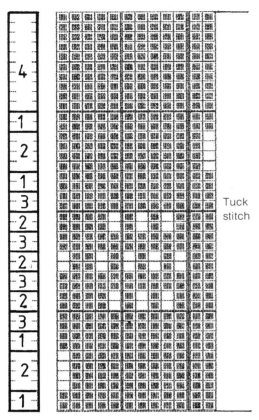

12 sts   40 rows

50b Patterncard

Yarn type
Colour 1 Main yarn plus lycra
Colour 2 Contrast yarn any thickness up to 4 ply
Colour 3 Fine yarn plus lycra
Colour 4 Main yarn any thickness up to 4 ply

Knitting instructions
1 Cast on the required number of stitches
2 Set the machine and carriage as appropriate
3 Knit in tuck stitch throughout changing the yarn as
  indicated

Different effects can be obtained by

1 altering the stocking stitch rows which are
knitted in elastic

2 increasing or decreasing the number of stitches
in each pattern.

List the design features which are of interest,
sketch them and convert to patterncards using the
method outlined above.

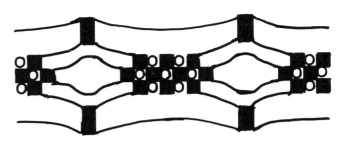

51a Incorrect placing of tuck blocks

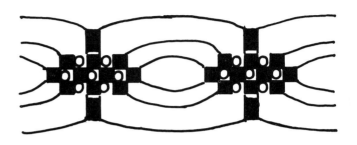

51b Correct placing of tuck blocks

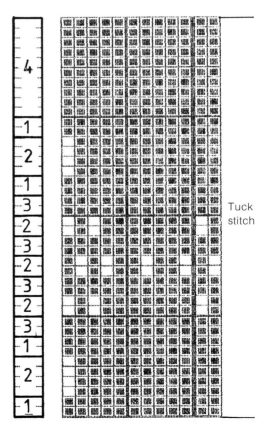

12 sts   40 rows

51d Patterncard for perfected cable

Yarn type and knitting instructions as for figure 50

50a Textured cable with incorrect placing of tuck blocks

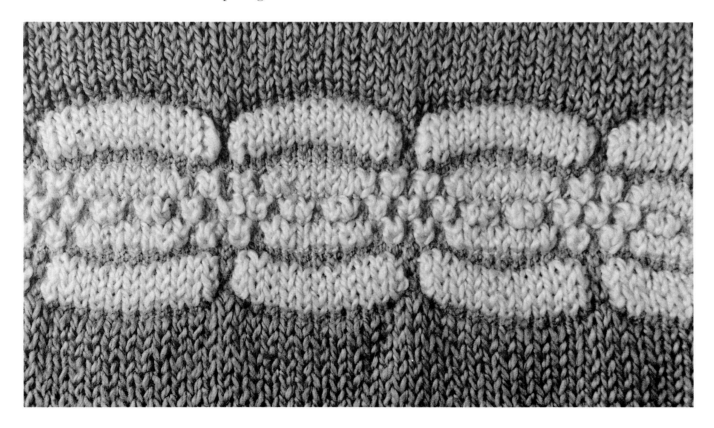

51c Perfected sample

Tuck lace

A tuck lace fabric is knitted in exactly the same way as an ordinary tuck fabric. The lace effect is created by leaving selected needles out of work. By eliminating certain sections of a basic patterncard a variety of designs can be produced.

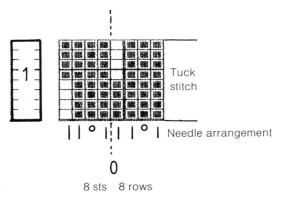

52a Patterncard with empty needles

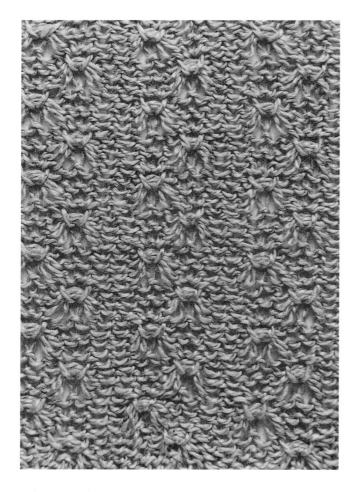

52b Knitted sample

Fabric definition

Depending on the thickness of the yarn used tuck lace produces a lightweight fabric with strands of yarn exposed across the gaps in the fabric left by the needles in non-working position. The knitside tends to have a raised texture and the purlside a stranded effect. Either side of the knitting can be used as the right side (figures 52 and 53).

Patterncard definition

The patterncards used for tuck lace are identical to those used for ordinary tuck stitch. Special cards can be designed. They have the empty needles marked on the patterncard (figure 53c).

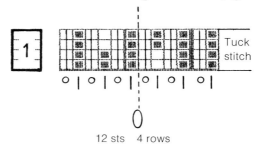

53c Patterncard with needle arrangement

Knitting method

Tuck lace is knitted in the same way as ordinary tuck stitch. However, because of the nature of the fabric certain precautions must be taken.

1 The work must be evenly weighted across the whole needlebed.

2 The end needle arrangement must be identical on both sides of the needlebed. If the end needle tucks on one side and not on the other the edges of the fabric will be of a different length.

3 On Brother punchcard machines which have end needle selection, the cams underneath the carriage must be disengaged. (See manual.) If this is not done, every time the carriage contacts a needle in working position it is thrown forward and knitted. It will not tuck. Owners of Brother electronic machines use KC II.

4 Always check the position of the centre of the patterncard and how it relates to the needle arrangement.

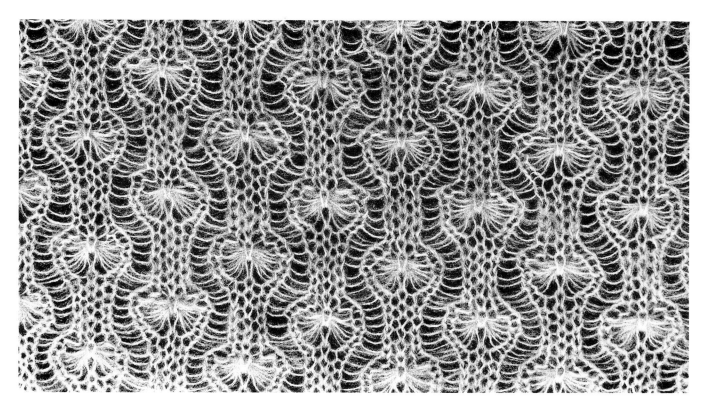

53a Tuck lace – knitside

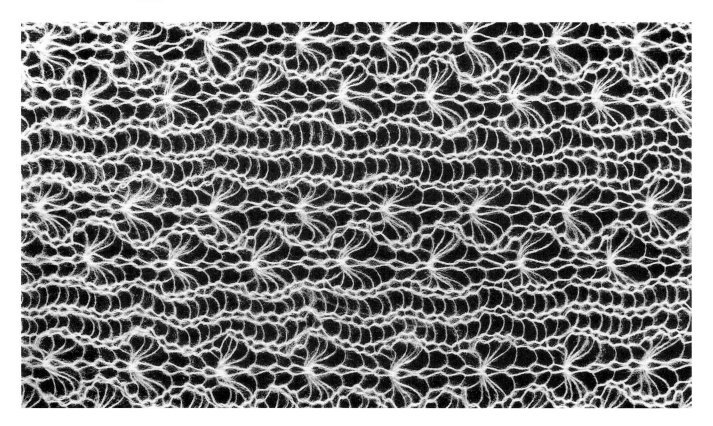

53b Tuck lace

Designing tuck lace patterncards

Patterncards for tuck lace tend to evolve from the basic patterncards rather than being designed. The possibilities are endless. Kate Armitage in her book *Card 3* (see the book list on page 141) created ten different tuck lace patterns from the one card.

New tuck lace patterns can be designed by varying the needle arrangement on the basic patterncards. The fabric can be totally altered by the number of needles out of work and where they are placed on the needlebed. Experiment with the basic cards and the various needle arrangements to gain an understanding of how the fabric is formed.

1 Try various needle arrangements, 1×1, 2×2, 2×1, etc, with the basic cards but be warned that the card with every alternate punching will not knit any tuck sections when used in conjunction with a 1×1 needle arrangement.

2 Use random needle arrangements. If certain sections of the pattern appeal they should be isolated and transferred to a patterncard.

3 Leave out of work the needles which are connected to the marked areas of the patterncard, i.e. those which are punched continually.

4 Leave some of the tuck sections out of work.

If the designing is carried out in a controlled way, i.e. each needle arrangement and patterncard number are recorded, the task is simplified. A design which seems to be a failure now may turn out to be the ideal solution to a problem in the future.

The fine yarn used in the illustration in figure 53 produces a gossamer-like fabric. However, any yarn up to a 3-ply thickness can be used. If the yarn is soft then the fabric will still be light and airy enough to be used for baby garments and shawls. Tuck lace has an old fashioned image created no doubt because in the early days, before the introduction of lace transfer carriages, it was the only means of producing a lightweight holey fabric on the knitting machine. It can be quite beautiful if the correct combination of yarn and patterncard is used. There are many sources for patterncards and needle arrangements for tuck lace. (See the book list on page 141.)

5 LACE

Fabric definition

Lace is a single-bed fabric with holes arranged in a decorative pattern. The holes are formed by transferring stitches from one needle to another in a planned sequence (figure 54).

There are two types of lace, simple and transfer. The other types of lace, punchlace and tuck lace referred to by machine knitters are lace-like. No actual stitch transfer takes place.

Fabric comparison

Lace widens and elongates a fabric. There are fewer stitches and rows to each centimetre than in stocking stitch.

Knitting methods

The various manufacturers have different methods of producing lace. The results are similar but not identical.

Brother and Toyota machines up to and including the 901

1 All lace worked on these machines is transfer lace.

2 Two carriages are required to produce the lace;

 a a lace carriage to select and transfer the stitches

 b a main carriage to knit the row.

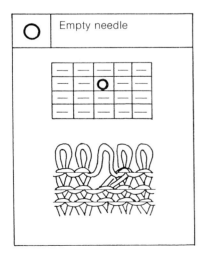 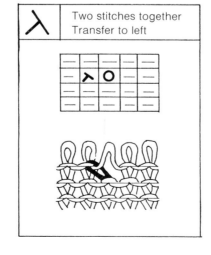 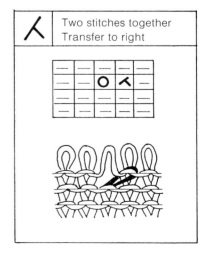

54a Lace symbols

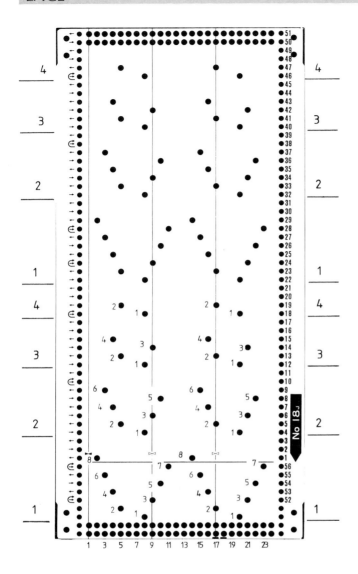

54b Typical lace punchcard. *Courtesy Brother*

54c Knitted sample

3 On the patterncard the arrows on the left of the card indicate the direction of the movement of the lace carriage (figure 54).

Knitmaster and Toyota 950 machines – Transfer lace
1 Only one carriage is needed.

2 The yarn must be removed to transfer the stitches in each sequence. It is replaced on the rows between the transfers.

3 The solid red markings, blue for the 270 and 370 fine knitter, on the right of the punchcard

indicate the movement of the lace carriage. The arrows on the left of the card indicate the direction of the movement of the lace carriage (figure 55).

Knitmaster and Toyota 950 machines – Simple lace
1 Only one carriage is used.

2 The lace is knitted by the movement of the carriage across the needlebed.

3 The carriage selects, transfers and knits in one movement.

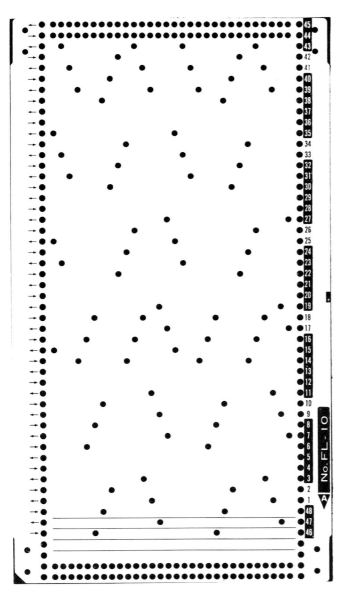

55 Transfer lace – Card FL 10. *Courtesy Knitmaster*

Punchcard definition

Transfer lace (possible on all machines with a lace carriage).

1 Mostly blank with occasional punched holes.

2 Any even number of rows in a sequence.

3 When the patterncards are knitted they produce a fabric which looks totally different from the markings on the card (figures 54b and 54c).

4 The arrows marked on the card indicate the direction of the lace carriage.

Since studying lace and the different types of cards used to produce it the explanation of how they work is simplified if transfer lace, with no more than four movements of the lace carriage, is separated from multiple transfer lace which has many more stitch movements. I shall refer to it as simple transfer lace.

Simple transfer lace
(possible on all machines with a lace carriage)

1 Mostly blank with occasional punched holes.

2 Only two or four rows in a sequence.

3 The patterncard produces a design similar to the card but the design is not as obvious as in simple one stroke lace (figure 56).

4 The arrows marked on the card indicate the direction of the lace carriage (figure 56).

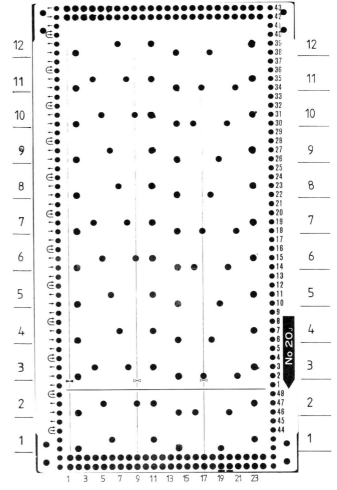

56a Simple transfer lace – Brother card 20J. *Courtesy Brother*

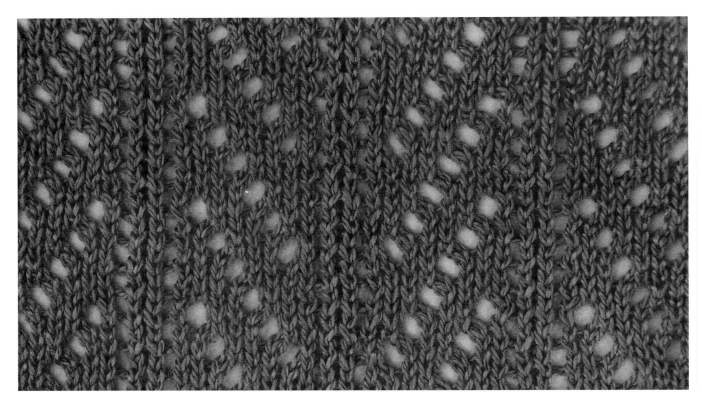

56b Knitted sample

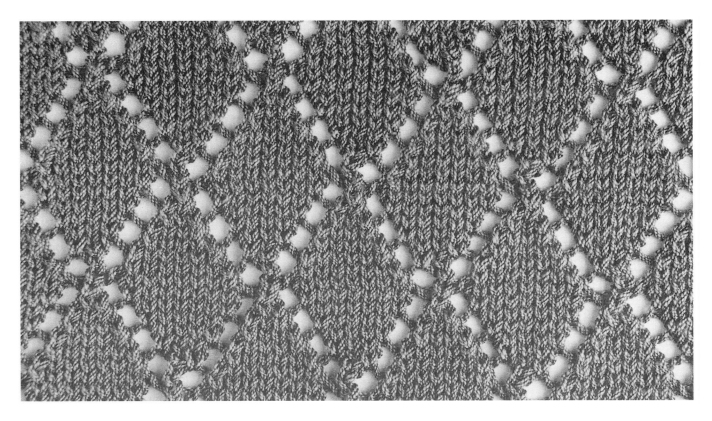

57b Knitmaster one stroke lace

Simple one stroke lace

(Knitmaster machines with a lace carriage and Toyota 950)

1 Can have large blank areas but has more holes than on transfer lace cards.

2 Each row of marking represents one row of selecting, transferring and knitting using the lace carriage.

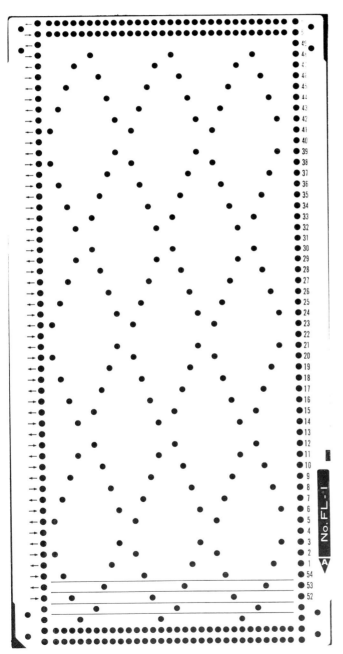

57a Card FL 1 – for Knitmaster fine knitter. *Courtesy Knitmaster*

3 Produces a pattern similar to the card markings (figure 57).

4 The arrows marked on the card indicate the direction of the lace carriage (figure 57).

Understanding the patterncard

Simple transfer lace and multiple transfer lace

Brother and Toyota

1 As a general rule the cards begin with a row of punched holes.

2 The punched holes enable the lace carriage to select the needles which will be transferred to form the pattern.

3 The first row of markings on a patterncard will select the needles to be transferred to the left.

4 The second row of markings in the same sequence will select the needles to be transferred to the right.

5 The blank rows between each sequence allow free movement of the lace carriage to either side of the machine to return the carriage to the left or to select the next row.

Knitmaster

1 As a general rule two rows are left blank at the beginning of a patterncard.

2 The punched holes enable the carriage to select, transfer and knit the needles required to form a pattern.

3 The first row of markings on a patterncard will select the needles to be transferred to the left.

4 The second row of markings in the same sequence will select the needles to be transferred to the right.

5 The blank rows between each sequence indicate that the yarn must be replaced into the feeder and that two rows must be knitted.

Simple lace

Toyota 950 and all Knitmaster machines with a lace carriage.

Simple or one stroke lace is knitted with a carriage which selects, transfers and knits in one movement of the lace carriage.

1 The first row of the patterncard is marked.

2 The punched holes enable the carriage to select, transfer and knit the needles required to form a pattern.

3 The first row of markings on a patterncard will select the needles to be transferred to the left.

4 The second row of markings will select the needles to be transferred to the right.

Note rules 3 and 4 apply for the length of the card. There are no sequences in simple lace as there are in transfer lace: the whole card is part of the pattern.

5 The arrows on the card indicate the direction of the movement of the lace carriage.

The outline given above is a summary of patterncards and the different methods used by each manufacturer to produce lace. The fabric is slightly different in that the strands of yarn across the holes can vary from one to two and the angle may be different. However, the fabric which is formed is always identified as lace.

It is possible to interchange the patterncards from different manufacturers. Bear in mind that:

1 Toyota machines, up to and including the 901, transfer stitches backwards, not forwards, as do Brother and Knitmaster lace carriages. To use the cards from these machines on a Brother or a Knitmaster machine simply turn the cards around, i.e. back to front.

2 To use Brother and Knitmaster transfer lace cards on the Toyota machines requires that the cards are reversed, i.e. front to back.

3 Knitmaster transfer lace cards can be identified by the solid marking on the right-hand side of the card. These cards can be used on Brother and Toyota machines **provided that there are only two unmarked (blank rows) between each pattern sequence**. If more than two blank rows are present beware! There is a section of simple lace in the midst of the transfer lace. The card can still be used but it must be adapted to convert the simple lace into simple transfer lace. Remember also that the selecting will occur on different numbered rows depending on which manufacturer's cards are being used on which type of machine.

4 Brother transfer lace cards can be used on the Knitmaster machines. Remember that the needle selection will occur on different numbered rows.

5 Simple lace cards can only be used on the machines indicated. To work them on the Brother and Toyota machines they will need to be converted to transfer lace.

Transferring a lace patterncard to a patternchart

When knitted many lace patterncards, particularly those for transfer lace, produce a pattern completely different from the one which appears on the card. The pattern can be converted into graphics to produce a chart which illustrates how the pattern will look on the purlside of the fabric. The process is a simple one if certain rules are followed. The chart marking for simple and simple transfer lace differs slightly from that of marking for transfer lace. The general guidelines listed below should help to simplify the process.

Guidelines to transferring a lace patterncard to graph paper

1 Study the international symbols for lace before trying to reproduce lace in diagram form.

2 Mark off on the graph paper an area the width of the chosen design.

3 Number every alternate row on the blank grid to ease the transfer of the design.

4 The holes and the direction of the stitch movement are marked on the chart. The blank rows on the chart which represent the purl row in hand knitting should be included to give the correct proportion to the design.

5 Each sequence of the patterncard represents one row on the chart.

6 Number the pattern rows of each sequence for ease of transfer.

7 Where only four movements of the lace carriage are worked the position of the punched hole/holes is marked on the graph paper together with the direction of transfer.

8 Where more than four movements of the lace carriage are required the direction of transfer is marked and, in addition, a dot. The dot is used in place of the empty needle symbol to simplify the chart. Continue in this way until the last punched hole of a sequence is reached. This final hole is marked on the graph sheet together with the empty needle symbol.

Note The resulting lace chart shows the purl side of the fabric.

Transferring a simple lace patterncard to graph paper

1 The first row of holes on the patterncard will transfer to the left. (Odd numbered rows to the left.)

2 The second row of holes on the patterncard will transfer to the right. (Even numbered rows to the right.)

3 Take note of the position of the needle/needles which will be selected first by the lace carriage.

Mark the graph sheet with an empty needle symbol, on row one, in the same stitch position as on the card.

4 Mark the direction of the transfer in the adjacent square.

5 Take note of the position of the next needle/needles to be selected by the lace carriage. Mark the graph sheet with an empty needle symbol, on row one, in the same stitch position as on the card.

6 Mark the direction of the transfer in the adjacent square.

7 Leave one row blank.

Repeat the above steps for the rest of the card.

There is not much point in converting these type of cards as the pattern produced is similar to the markings on the card. The only advantage is that the direction of transfer is indicated.

Transferring simple transfer lace patterncards to graph paper

Choose a card with only four movements of the lace carriage, say Brother card 20J (23D) (figure 56). The card is marked out in sequence. Each sequence is numbered. Transfer the design to a chart. The patterncard is based on a square grid. Transfer your design onto proportional graph paper to give a better idea of how the knitted fabric will look.

1 The first row of holes on the patterncard will transfer to the left. (Odd numbered rows of each sequence to the left.)

2 The second row of holes on the patterncard will transfer to the right. (Even numbered rows of each sequence to the right.)

3 Take note of the position of the needle/needles which will be selected first by the lace carriage. Mark the graph sheet with an empty needle symbol, on row one, in the same stitch position as on the card.

4 Mark the direction of the transfer in the adjacent square.

5 Take note of the position of the next needle/needles to be selected by the lace carriage. Mark the graph sheet with an empty needle symbol, on row one, in the same stitch position as on the card.

6 Mark the direction of the transfer in the adjacent square.

7 Leave one row blank.

Repeat for the rest of the card beginning a new row on the graph sheet for each new sequence (figure 58).

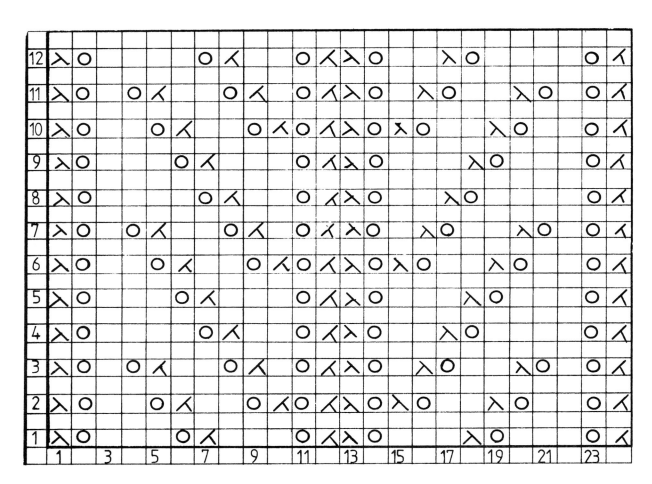

58a (i) First sequence
(ii) Order of transfer
(iii) First row of chart

58b Completed chart

Transferring transfer lace patterncards to graph paper

1 The first row of holes on the patterncard will transfer to the left.

2 The next row of holes on the patterncard will transfer to the right.

3 Take note of the position of the needle/needles which will be selected first by the lace carriage.

Mark the graph sheet with a dot in the same stitch position as on the patterncard (figure 59a).

4 Mark the direction of transfer in the adjacent square.

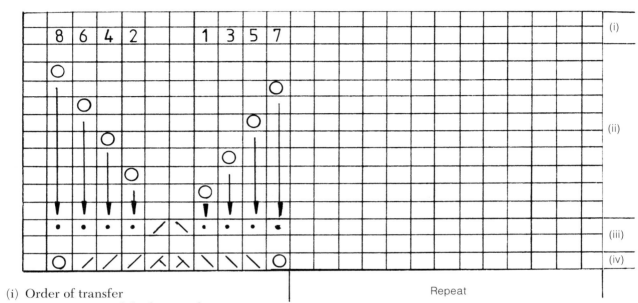

59a (i) Order of transfer
  (ii) First sequence of the lace card
  (iii) Marking the dots
  (iv) First row of chart

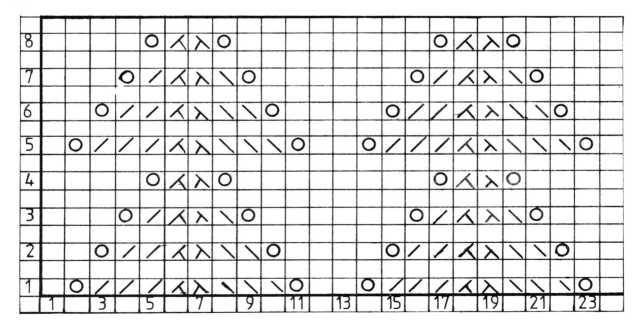

59b Completed chart

5 Take note of the position of the needle/needles which will be selected next by the lace carriage. Mark the graph sheet with a dot in the same stitch position as on the patterncard but on the same row of the chart as in step 3.

6 Mark the direction of transfer in the adjacent square.

7 Continue in this way until all the markings in the sequence have been transferred to the graph paper (figure 59a).

Note The direction of transfer will cover the dot marked for the previous stitch movement. It will be seen that the last dot marked cannot be covered by a direction of transfer symbol. Mark this square with the empty needle symbol (figure 59a).

Repeat until all the sequences on the patterncard have been transferred (figure 59b).

Notes for guidance

1 Isolate each lace sequence for the length of the patterncard. Mark in numerical order. This helps to identify the pattern row on the chart (figure 54b).

2 Mark each row of each sequence on the patterncard in numerical order. This helps to identify the direction of transfer (figure 54b).

3 Each complete sequence consists of an even number of rows.

a Odd numbered rows in a sequence will transfer to the left.
b Even numbered rows in a sequence will transfer to the right.

4 Where there are only two rows in a sequence mark the punched holes as for simple transfer lace, i.e. mark the empty needle position and the direction of transfer at the same time. This usually completes a series of multiple transfers.

Converting a lace chart to a punchcard

Once the skill of converting a patterncard to a chart has been mastered it is essential to learn how to change it back to a patterncard. In the initial experiment it is an advantage to use commercial patterncards as it is easier to check that the correct procedure is being used for the conversion.

1 The card can be knitted without fear of faults to confirm that the chart is correct.

2 When the chart has been translated back to a patterncard (on the graph paper) the design should be identical to the original patterncard. This confirms that the process has been successfully carried out. If the design is different from the original something is wrong.

Guidelines

1 Brother owners begin to mark the design on the first row of the patterncard.

Note The first row of the patterncard is the row directly above the overlap holes, **not** the row marked 1 on the patterncard (figure 54b).

2 Knitmaster owners begin to mark the design on the third row of the patterncard.

Note The third row of the patterncard is the third row directly above the overlap holes, **not** the row marked 3 on the patterncard (figure 55).

3 Each row of the chart represents a complete sequence of lace carriage markings (figure 59a).

4 Where a pattern is repeated across a patterncard the corresponding stitch in the repeat pattern is also marked.

Conversion of a simple transfer lace chart to a patterncard

Return to the chart of the Brother card which was transferred to proportional graph paper and convert it back to a patterncard using graph paper rather than a patterncard (figure 58). As this patterncard has only four movements of the lace carriage the conversion is not difficult.

1 Identify the needle/needles which need moving to the left. Mark the stitch on the patterncard (graph paper) (figure 60).

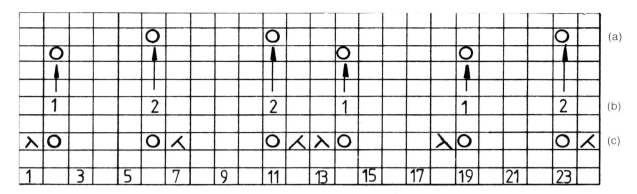

60a First row of chart from figure 58
60b Order of transfer
60c First sequence of patterncard in figure 56

2 Identify the needle/needles which need moving to the right. Mark the stitch on to the patterncard (graph paper) (figure 60).

3 Make sure that every mark on the first row of the chart has been recorded on the patterncard (figure 60).

4 Repeat for each row marked on the chart.

5 Check your graph paper patterncard against the original pattern card. It should match exactly.

Conversion of multiple transfer lace charts to patterncards

The patterncard used above is quite simple to transfer, the more intricate patterns need a little more care and slightly different rules apply.

Guidelines to converting multiple transfer charts to patterncards

1 Brother owners begin to mark the design on the first row of the patterncard.

Note The first row of the patterncard is the row directly above the overlap holes, **not** the row marked 1 on the patterncard.

2 Knitmaster owners begin to mark the design on the third row of the patterncard.

Note The third row of the patterncard is the third row directly above the overlap holes, **not** the row marked 3 on the patterncard.

3 Each row of the chart represents a complete sequence of lace carriage markings.

4 Only one stitch in each pattern can be moved at a time. However, if the pattern is repeated across a patterncard then the corresponding stitch in the repeat pattern is also marked on the chart.

5 Each marking/stitch is allocated a row to itself on the pattern card.

Transferring multiple lace charts

1 The marking furthest away from the empty needle symbol on the side which needs transferring to the left is the first to be marked on the patterncard (figure 61).

2 The marking furthest away from the empty needle symbol on the side which needs transferring to the right is marked on the next row of the patterncard. To make the conversion easier it is useful to mark the order of transfer on the chart (figure 61).

3 Continue in this manner gradually working towards the empty needle symbol. Reaching this/these marking(s) indicates the end of the stitch movements for this particular chart row.

4 Leave two rows blank on the card.

5 Repeat the sequence with the appropriate markings on the next row of the chart until the whole chart has been converted.

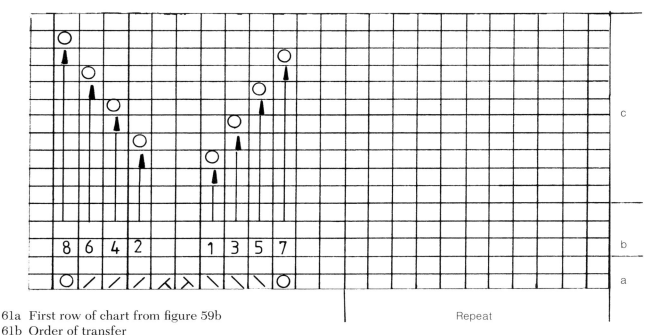

61a First row of chart from figure 59b
61b Order of transfer
61c First sequence of patterncard

Designing lace cards

There are three ways of designing lace

1 Adapting commercial patterncards.

2 Converting handknitted lace patterns.

3 Creating new designs by using charts.

Adapting commercial lace card

1 Lace patterns with varying widths.

   a Use different combinations of the basic lace designs.
   b Repeat the same pattern a number of times then introduce a new one.
   c Move the pattern halfway across.
   d Combine two lace patterns across a patterncard taking care that these patterns do not overlap.

2 Lace patterns with the same pattern base.

   a Try lace patterns with same pattern base one after another – interesting shapes can be formed.
   b Repeat the same pattern a number times then introduce a second.

   c Move the pattern halfway across.
   d Combine two lace patterns across a patterncard taking care that these patterns do not overlap.

3 Transfer the lace charts from the Japanese magazines. Many of these lace charts are very beautiful.

Owners of punchcard machines have more restrictions placed on their lace design work in this particular section than owners of electronic machines; the twenty four stitch pattern base overrides any other consideration. It is still possible to create new twenty four stitch lace patterns by combining patterns in the way described above but, before wasting time punching cards with these new combinations, it is worth translating the selected patterncards onto a lace chart to see the effect. Do make sure that the design is repeated at least twice both vertically and horizontally to eliminate any pattern faults.

Creating new lace designs from old established patterns is a simple matter for owners of electronic machines, particularly those with a PPD. There are no pattern width restrictions and no extra marking as the patterns can be placed anywhere on the grid. It is still an advantage to translate the design to a patternchart to spot potential design faults.

Without a PPD the designs must be marked out on a mylar sheet before being knitted.

No matter which method is used remember that, when knitting the design, any faults which occur in the knitting can be located on the purlside not on the faceside of the fabric.

Hand knitted lace conversion

Converting hand knitted lace patterns for use on the machine is possible provided the lace is of a simple straightforward design. Ready-made charts are the easiest to translate. Hand knitted and charted lace patterns can be found in various publications, such as Mary Thomas's *Knitting Patterns*, Barbara Walker's *Charted Knitted Designs*, *Burda* pattern books and many of the continental magazines. Unfortunately the symbols used are not standard but as a key is given it is not too difficult to convert them to a patterncard

using the details set out on pages 74–75 for transferring lace patterncharts to patterncards. If the symbols are obscure then translate them onto a patternchart before attempting to mark out a card.

Where a more complicated lace is involved it is not possible to do a straightforward conversion. Any lace with purl stitches on the knit side is only possible if hand tooling or the garter carriage is to be used (figure 62). On the machine we are only able to transfer stitches in front of the stitch on the needle with the purlside of the knitting facing the knitter. To reproduce the textured effect achieved when hand knitting would entail hand tooling. The choice is up to the individual. However, if it is speed which concerns you then this method is to be avoided.

Machine knitters are unlikely to find the idea of increasing in the middle of a row a practical proposition and, where this is indicated, it is better to find an alternative machine method to produce a similar effect.

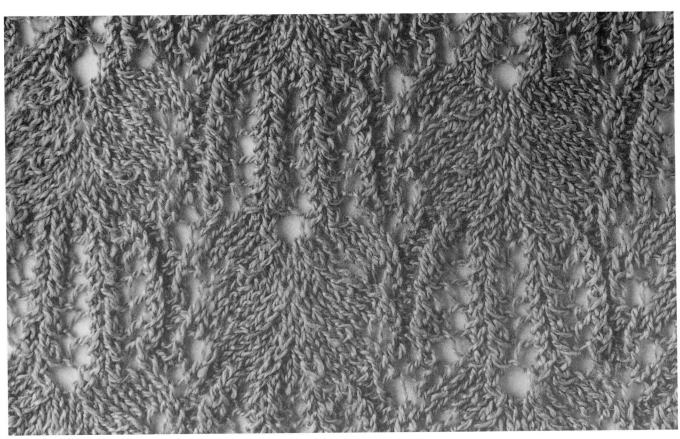

62 Hand knitted frost flowers lace

When knitting lace by hand there is no pattern width restriction. The same applies to owners of electronic machines. The owners of punchcard machines will find that many lace patterns fit into the twenty four stitch discipline without much difficulty.

The exercises which have been worked should have given an understanding of how to convert the design to a chart and then to a patterncard. For more details see *The Technique of Lace* by Kathleen Kinder.

Creating lace by using charts

The previous exercises have been planned to give you an insight into the workings of the lace carriage and the relationship between the patterncard and the needlebed. This knowledge can be put to good use to create your own lace patterns.

1 Learn to recognize the type of pattern produced by the basic symbols from the international symbol chart. These are the equivalent of your basic patterncards in other stitches (figure 63).

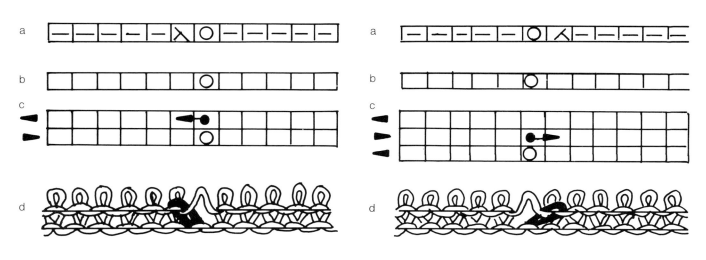

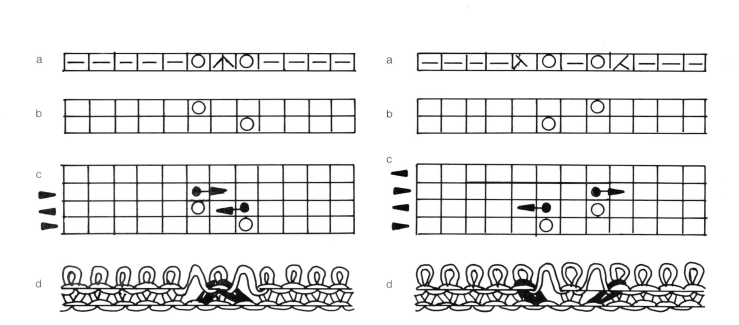

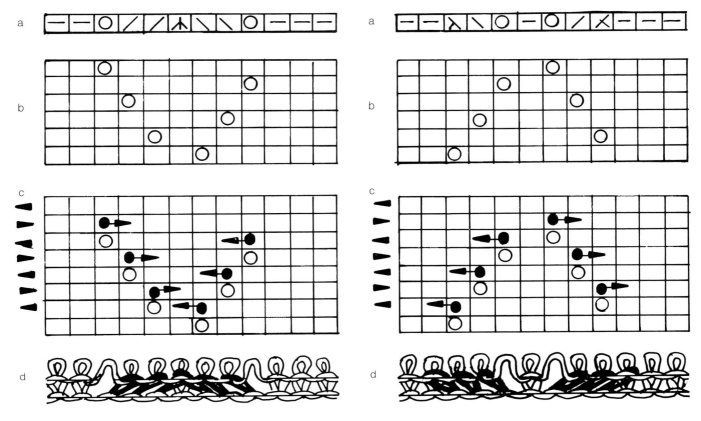

Multiple transfers   Multiple transfers

a

b

c

d

○	Empty needle
╱◦	Two stitches together Transfer to right
╲◦	Two stitches together Transfer to left
╱	Transfer to right
╲	Transfer to left
⋏	Three stitches together
●▬▶	Selected stitch Transfer to right
◀▬●	Selected stitch Transfer to left

63 Diagrams of basic lace patterns (left and above)
a The chart marking
b Patterncard translation
c Direction of travel of lace carriage
d Purlside of fabric

2 Mark the pattern on a proportional grid leaving one row blank between each lace sequence.

3 Transfer the patternchart to a patterncard as detailed earlier in this chapter (figure 64).

Combining commercial lace cards with original and/or adapted lace patterns

There are more creative ways of using commercial cards. Many of the traditional lace patterns used on the machine have been transferred from hand knitted designs and many of the most attractive hand knitted laces are combinations of basic lace patterns as well as the traditional designs. A good example of this is 'Frost Flowers' from Barbara Walker's book *A Treasury of Knitting Patterns* (figure 62).

When sweaters in a similar machine knitted version of the pattern appeared in a well-known chain store, the desire to create a card for the domestic knitting machine proved overwhelming.

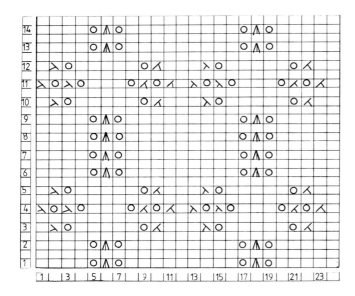

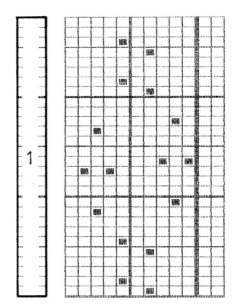

64a New simple transfer lace chart – two repeats
horizontally and vertically

64c Patterncard

Yarn type

Any yarn suitable for lace knitting

Knitting instructions

1 Cast on the required number of stitches
2 Set the machine and carriage as appropriate
3 Knit the pattern.
4 Repeat for the desired length

64b Knitted sample

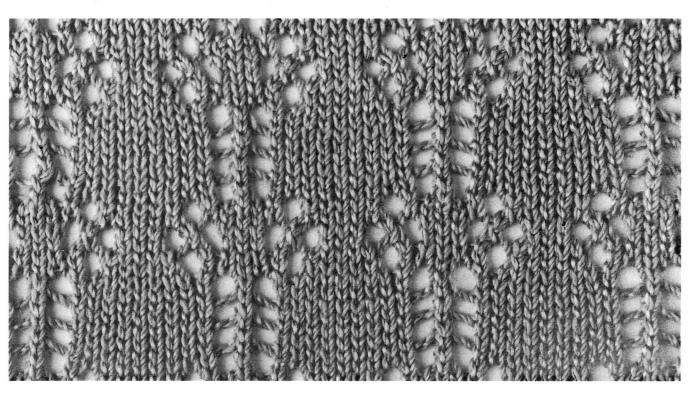

The card was originally designed by trial and error as the idea of designing lace by charts was not normal practice. With the advent of the City and Guilds of London Institute Machine Knitting course, students are required to produce new lace patterns plus evidence of their evolution. How much easier it is to be able to mark out a chart indicating exactly what is required, transfer the design to a patterncard or the punchcard pattern design and knit it.

Observe the hand knitted version in figure 62. The design can be split into three sections.

1 The cable effect lace.

2 The fagotting.

3 The purl stitches.

Unfortunately because of the width of the pattern it is only suitable for electronic machines.

1 The cable effect lace with its stitch movement sweeping across the design is the main feature which must have given this pattern its name. (Barbara Walker says that this is not its real name but the design is so suggestive of frost that it

65b Knitted sample

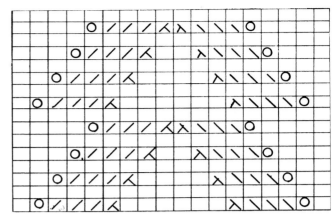

65a Chart for cable lace

would seem to be ideal.) The lace pattern selected for this section is from a chart in an old magazine (figure 65). The cable effect produced by the design needs to be used as a single motif. When the pattern is knitted across the full width of a fabric it is difficult to realize that the cable needs to be altered to make the stitches lean towards the centre of the section in order to imitate the hand knitted version which we are trying to reproduce. The pattern is not as compact as the hand knitted version because it is worked on every alternate row as opposed to every row in the original.

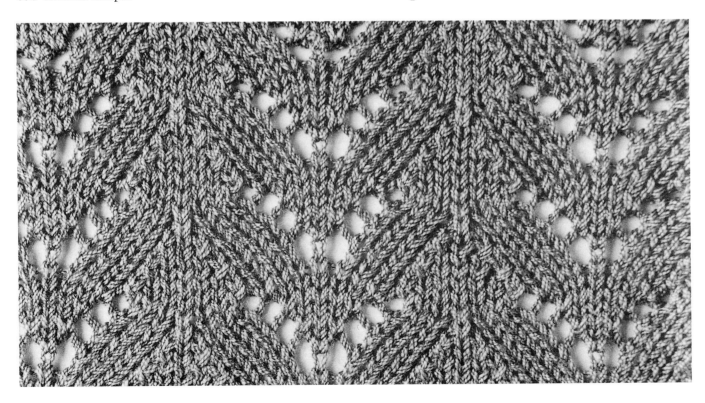

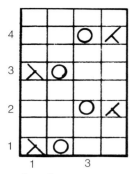

66 Chart for alternating lace

transferred to the left on one sequence and the second stitch is transferred to the right on the following sequence, the two knit rows between these movements prevent this happening (figure 66).

3 As already discussed, the purl sections cannot be included unless a garter carriage or hand tooling is to be used. It would be difficult to include the two purl stitches at each side of the cable lace even if the patterncard was redesigned. The garter carriage cannot cope with two stitches on one needle. The first knit row will have to be worked with the main carriage, the second row with the garter carriage. Difficulties can arise when using this method as there are three carriages on the machine! The individual has to decide whether the need to remove one carriage to allow room for another is worth the time and effort to incorporate two purl stitches at each side of the cable lace.

2 The fagotting and corded sections are composed of a combination of basic and adapted basic patterns. The corded section makes use of part of Brother card 20J (figure 56). The fagotting requires a slight adaptation to the basic mesh. Alternating holes are required in the centre of the design. Stitches which are next to each other cannot normally be transferred as they leave two adjacent needles empty. If, however, one stitch is

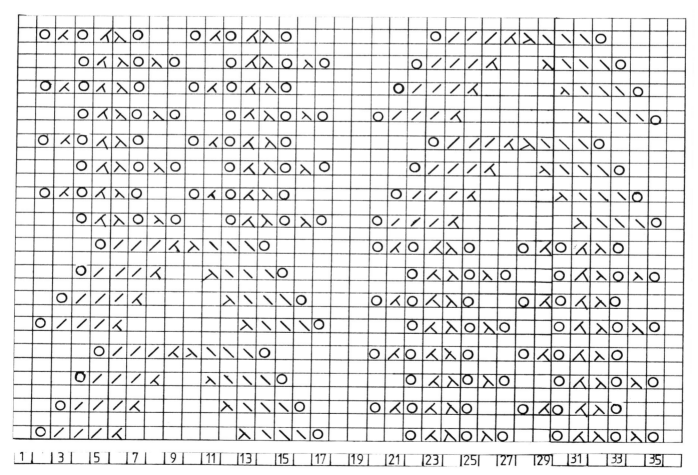

67a Chart for Frost Flowers

Creating the patternchart

Now that each section has been designed the patterncharts must be amalgamated. A design is usually placed in the centre of a patterncard but in this case it is easier to place the cable lace on one side and the other lace next to it. This arrangement must be used in order to display the two sections of the pattern quite clearly and to see the way in which they relate to each other. The pattern can be moved to the centre of the needlebed when the machine is programmed.

First mark out the cable effect then the fagotting and corded section. The last section is simple transfer lace and can be marked on any line of the patterncard as long as the transfer is in the appropriate direction. It is simpler to place it at the beginning of each sequence in order that the knitting can be checked for dropped stitches (figure 67).

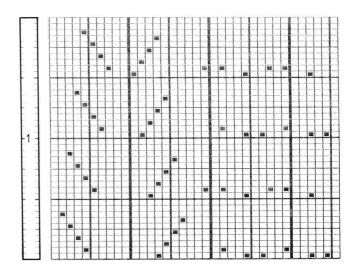

67c Patterncard for Frost Flowers

Yarn type
Any yarn suitable for lace

Knitting instructions
1 Cast on the required number of stitches
2 Set the machine and carriage as appropriate
3 Knit the pattern three times then shift it 18 stitches across the needlebed
4 Knit the pattern three times then move it back to its original position. Repeat for the desired length

67b Knitted sample

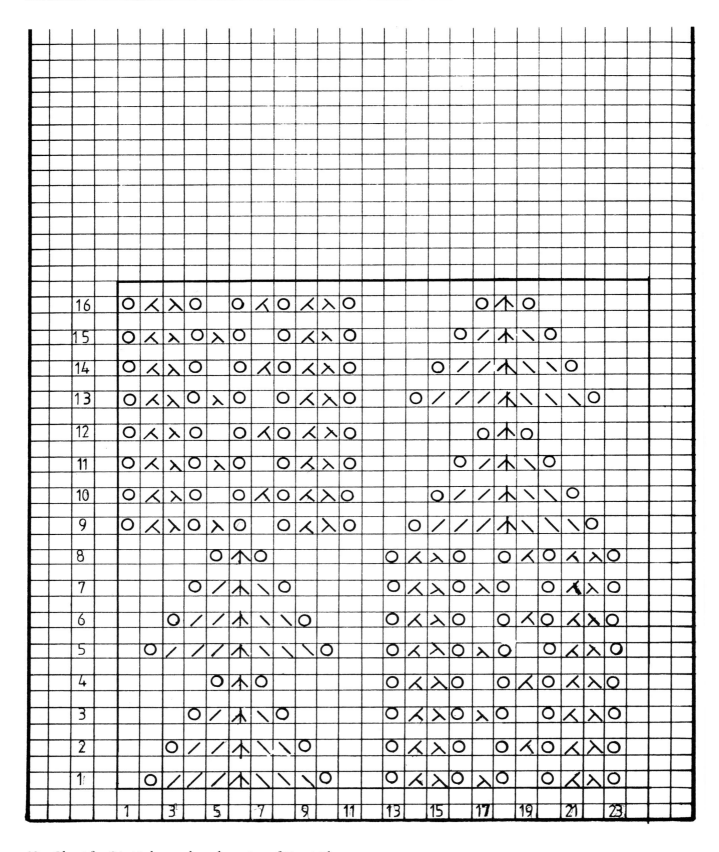

68a Chart for 24 stitch punchcard version of Frost Flowers

Conversion from lace patternchart to patterncard

Follow the instructions given on page 75.

The 'Frost Flowers' design just created is too wide for a twenty four stitch punchcard machine but there is no reason why new skills cannot be used. Why not chart out a smaller design? The cable section can remain the same, only the cording and fagotting need to be reduced. Remember that it is better to chart two repeats both vertically and horizontally to see where the faults in the pattern are likely to occur (figure 68a).

Lace is not as complicated as it first appears. Its mystique is certainly reduced once the skill of marking charts has been mastered.

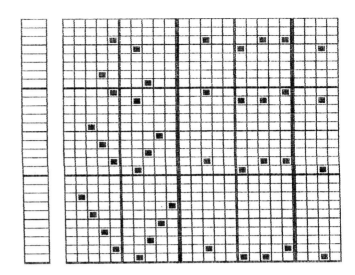

68c Frost Flower patterncard

Yarn type
Any yarn up to 4 ply thickness

Knitting instructions
1 Cast on the required number of stitches
2 Set the machine and carriage as appropriate
3 Knit the pattern three times then shift it 12 stitches across the needlebed
4 Knit the pattern three times more then move it back to its original position. Repeat steps 3 and 4 for the desired length

68b Knitted sample

6 RIBBER AND GARTER STITCHES

The ribber and the garter carriage are attachments which can be added to a single-bed knitting machine to increase its potential. There is a ribber available for all single-bed machines. The garter carriage is available for Brother machines only, from the 860 upwards. Both attachments form a fabric with knit and purl stitches but they differ in the way in which they produce it.

A garter stitch fabric is knitted automatically, independently of the operator, on the single-bed machine. The standard ribs for welts, which are usually knitted on the ribbing attachment with the ribber on full pitch, can be produced on the garter carriage as well but they are more successful using thicker yarns as the needle gauge remains constant.

Fabrics knitted with the ribbing attachment are more complex. They can be divided into different types, each requiring a single-bed machine with a ribbing attachment or a double-bed machine.

1 Double ribs which are produced on both beds to give a fabric with an industrial appearance, i.e. 2 × 1, full needle rib and long stitch. The ribber is set to half pitch to reduce the gauge and allow the needles on each bed to work without clashing.

2 Patterned fabrics using colour and texture combined with the pattern facilities of the main bed. These fabrics can only be knitted when the ribber is attached. The ribber is set to half pitch to reduce the gauge and allow the needles on each bed to work without clashing (figure 69).

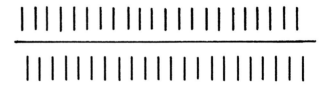

69a Ribber set to half pitch

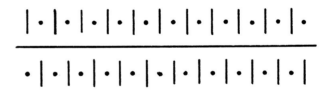

69b Ribber set to full pitch

The ribber can be used in conjunction with Fair Isle, tuck and slip patterncards. Each attains a new identity.

Fair Isle

1 Double jacquard.

2 Lined and quilted jacquard.

3 Blister stitch.

All these techniques use the double jacquard setting on the electronic machines. The cards are designed to separate the main and contrast yarn to allow them to be knitted independently.

Slip

1 Multicoloured knitting.

2 Ripple stitch.

Both techniques use the slip setting. The cards are again designed to separate each colour to allow them to be knitted independently but, depending on the stitch type, floats can occur in the fabric.

Tuck

1 Tuck ribs.

2 Mock Aran.

Tuck ribs and mock Aran patterns can use the same patterncards as are used for single-bed work. However, it is possible to design specific patterncards for them.

For other advanced ribber techniques see the book list on page 141.

Ribber stitches – Fair Isle

Note. The Fair Isle cams cannot be used when the ribber arm is attached. The word Fair Isle has been used to indicate coloured knitting.

Double jacquard

Fabric definition

Double jacquard is a two-colour, double-thickness, float-free fabric with patterning on the face side. The reverse side can vary from two colour dots or stripes to pintucks depending on the setting of the ribber carriage. It is the double-bed equivalent of Fair Isle (figure 70).

Patterncard definition

Patterncards designed for use with the double jacquard setting on the electronic machines are identical to those used for Fair Isle. The machine converts the design automatically when the double jacquard button is used.

The patterncards used for double jacquard fabrics on punchcard machines have an unusual appearance. No distinct pattern is visible and the

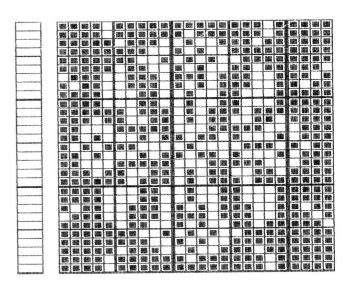

70a Patterncard for double jacquard

Yarn type
Colour 1 Background yarn
Colour 2 Main yarn
Fine yarns of similar thickness

70b Knitted sample

image is blurred because each colour is allocated a row to itself on the punchcard (figure 73b). The balance between the punched and unpunched areas is irrelevant as each square on every two row sequence must be marked to avoid a pattern fault (figure 71).

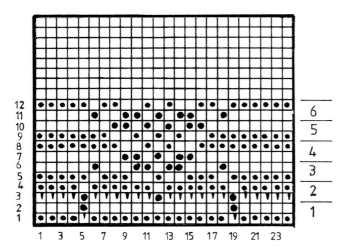

V   Direction of stitch movement when knitting

71 Checking double jacquard

Knitting method

Single-bed Fair Isle is knitted using a special form of slip stitch which allows two colours to be knitted in one row. Double jacquard uses the slip setting but the colours are knitted separately to enable the ribber to take up the floats which would form if the pattern were knitted on the single bed. Only one colour is knitted at a time.

Row 1

a The needles in contact with the blank areas of the card are not selected; they remain in working position. When the slip setting is used on the single bed these needles are bypassed by the carriage leaving a strand of yarn across the block of non-selected needles. When the ribber is attached, and set to knit over every needle on every row, the non-selected needles are bypassed as before, but the ribber stitches knit the yarn which would have formed a float if the fabric had been knitted on the single bed.

b The needles in contact with the punched areas of the card are selected to upper working position. These areas will knit the background colour on the main bed. Every needle on the ribber bed will knit in the background colour.

Row 2

a The needles in contact with the blank areas of the card which are not selected on this row are the areas of the card which were knitted on row 1, section b.

b The needles in contact with the punched areas of the card which are selected to upper working position will knit the contrast colour on the main bed. These areas are the ones not knitted on row 1, section a. Every needle on the ribber bed will knit in the contrast colour.

After the selection of the second row the knitting is carried out in two row sequences, i.e. four rows are worked to produce two actual rows of knitting; two rows in colour 2, two rows in colour 1.

Each row of the sequence may be different.

The special marking of punchcards for double jacquard, lined and quilted jacquard and blister stitch illustrates the way in which the electronic machines interpret the mylar sheet.

Studying an adapted punchcard highlights the fact that, unlike slip and tuck stitch on the single bed, any area left blank on one row will be knitted on the next row to avoid any fabric distortion. The punched areas allow the knitter to select the desired colour and place it where required. With the main carriage set to slip the blank areas are bypassed until, on the following row, the needle positions are reversed and the second colour slots into place.

Duomatics

The same method of selection occurs on the duomatics, with the deco set to four, but the cards are not marked in any special way. The arrow keys and the pushers alternate the selection. However, each sequence of two rows is identical because the deco can only select one way, from right to left, therefore every row must be repeated.

Creating double jacquard patterncards

Any Fair Isle patterncard can be converted to double jacquard. Patterncards with long floats lend themselves very well to the adaptation as the floats are eliminated when the design is knitted. The patterncard from chapter 2, figure 20, which was converted to twenty four stitches, is ideal. However, the design markings need to be reversed as, in its original form, the background is punched. Figure 72 gives the adapted patterncard. It is marked on a squared grid as the design has already been developed.

Converting a Fair Isle patterncard to double jacquard

The background and contrast colours must be separated. The blank areas of the patterncard form the background colour. The punched areas of the patterncard form the contrast colour.

1 Mark the patterncard off into two row sequences (figure 72).

Note The design has an odd number of rows. Add one row to complete the last two row sequence.

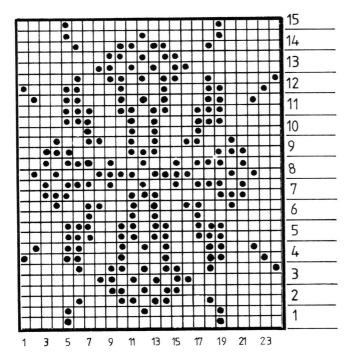

72 Patterncard marked in reverse

2 Number each sequence to allow easy identification should mistakes occur when transferring the design (figure 72).

3 Leave the first row of the grid blank (figure 73a).

4 Mark the blank grid, above the first empty row, into two row sequences (figure 73a).

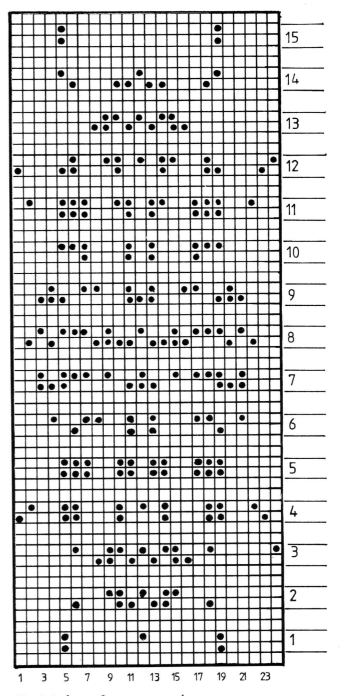

73a Markings for contrast colour

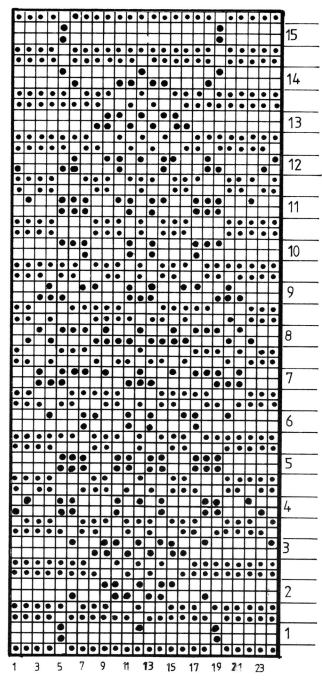

| | Background yarn |
| | Contrast yarn |

73b Completed patterncard

5 Number the first and every subsequent alternate sequence (figure 73a).

6 Mark each two row numbered sequence from the patterncard on the corresponding numbered row of the grid (figure 73a).

Continue with step 6 until the whole pattern is marked on the grid. The contrast (pattern) rows are now completed (figure 73a).

7 On the first row and the following alternate unnumbered two row sequences of the grid mark in the background areas. This is achieved by marking every square not filled by the contrast pattern rows (figure 73b).

Now that the design has been marked the above two row sequence of marking can be disregarded. It was only used to ease the transfer of the design from a Fair Isle card to a double jacquard card. Two row sequences do apply but in a different order.

Rows 1 and 2; 3 and 4, etc, form their own two row sequences. To check that the marking is correct, every square across the width of the pattern on the grid of these new sequences must be marked (figure 71). If it is not, then the pattern will be incorrect.

Designing double jacquard patterncards

Patterncards designed for use as double jacquard fabrics are planned on proportional graph paper. A double jacquard fabric requires four movements of the carriage to produce two rows of knitting. This can elongate the design depending on the setting of the ribber.

Follow the instructions for creating Fair Isle designs given in chapter 2 remembering that design restrictions are not as crucial as there will be no floats.

After perfecting the design follow the instructions for converting a Fair Isle patterncard to double jacquard.

Lined jacquard

Lined jacquard is an extension of double jacquard. The cards are marked in a similar way in that the colours are separated. They differ because a double jacquard fabric is knitted using both beds together. When knitting lined jacquard the front and back beds knit separately except for the odd stitch which connects the fabric.

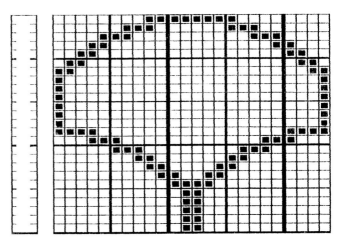

Fabric definition

A lined jacquard fabric is of double thickness. The front and back are separate except for the occasional stitch which holds the fabric together. Pockets are formed in the shape of the planned design (figure 74). Lined jacquard can be knitted in one or two colours. When using more than one colour the faceside of the fabric is multicoloured. The reverse side is knitted in the contrast yarn. The colour on the faceside of lined jacquard is more intense than in double jacquard as there is no 'show through' of the second yarn.

Patterncard definition

The patterncards designed to produce lined jacquard on the electronic machines are identical to those used for Fair Isle. They are predominantly blank with the markings outlining simple shapes (figure 75).

74 Knitted sample of lined jacquard

75 Fair Isle patterncard for lined jacquard

The patterncards used for knitting lined jacquard fabrics on punchcard machines have a similar appearance to those for double jacquard. No distinct pattern is visible and the image is blurred because each colour is allocated a row to itself on the punchcard. However, instead of the colour being marked two rows at a time, eg two rows of colour 1, two rows of colour 2 (figure 73c), the colours are separated as before but each sequence is marked separately, eg colour 1, colour 2; colour 1, colour 2, for the length of the card (figure 76).

Knitting method

Electronic machines

Lined jacquard can be knitted in two ways on the electronic machines. The fabric is always knitted in two row, two colour sequences with the tension evenly balanced between both beds but the patterncards are marked in a different way.

A Using a Fair Isle patterncard, the double jacquard setting and elongation (figure 75).

B Using the same type of patterncard marking as the punchcard machine (figure 76).

Method A
The fabric is knitted in two row, two colour sequences. Using the double jacquard, select the main colour and cast on. The pattern memory must be selected from left to right to allow a single row of background yarn to be knitted before the regular yarn change takes place.

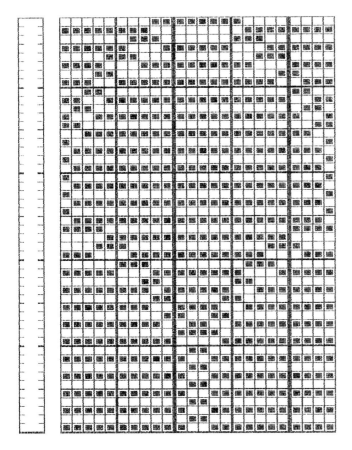

76a Lined jacquard marking. Complete patterncard.
Knit with the machine set to elongation

1 After the initial selection knit one row from
right to left with the main carriage and the ribber
carriage set to slip both ways.

2 Change to the contrast yarn, knit two rows with
the main carriage set to slip and the ribber
carriage set to knit both ways.

3 Change to the main yarn, knit two rows with
the main carriage and the ribber carriage set to
slip both ways.

Repeat steps 2 to 3 for the length of the
patterncard.

76b Double marked lined jacquard patterncard

Yarn type
Colours 1 and 2 Any yarn up to 3 ply thickness

Knitting instuctions
See text

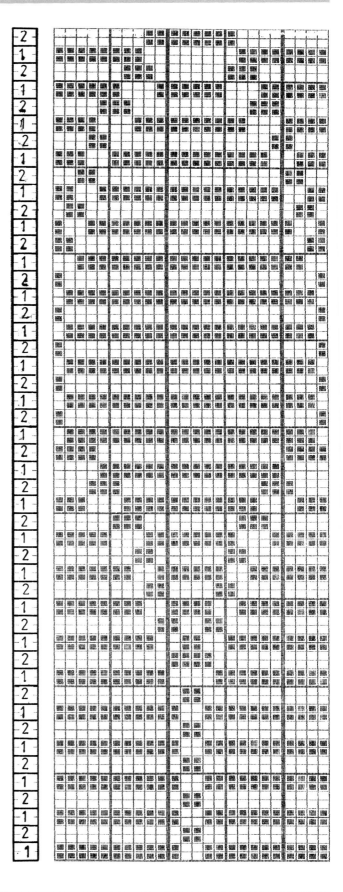

Method B
Follow the instructions for punchcard machines.

Punchcard machines

Mark the patterncard as indicated in figure 76.

1 Cast on in background yarn, knit a few rows. With the carriage on the right knit one row from right to left to select the first row.

2 Knit two rows in the background yarn with the carriage set to slip and the ribber set to slip both ways.

3 Change to the contrast yarn. Knit 2 rows with the main carriage set to slip and the ribber carriage set to knit both ways.

4 Change to the background yarn. Knit two rows with the carriage set to slip and the ribber set to slip both ways.

The following guidelines should be noted.

1 The main carriage is set to slip throughout.

2 The ribber is set to knit for two rows then to slip for two rows. Make sure that the ribber is on slip when most needles are selected. This keeps the fabric separate.

3 The yarn tension must be evenly balanced to produce a smooth fabric which lies flat.

77a Simple pattern shape
77b Grid marked in sequence with the blank areas of the pattern shape marked
77c Punched areas of card marked

Creating lined jacquard patterncards

Lined jacquard patterncards should be designed on proportional paper.

1 Select a simple pattern shape (figure 77a).

2 Mark the pattern grid in two row sequences (figure 77b).

3 Mark the blank sections of the design onto the first row of each sequence.

4 Mark the marked sections of the design onto the second row of each sequence.

Repeat steps 3 and 4 for the length of the design.

Quilted jacquard

Quilted jacquard is designed and knitted using the same method as lined jacquard. The texturing on the surface of the quilted fabric is created by knitting with an uneven tension. The crumpled surface can be left as it is or pieces of wadding, the same shape as the pocket, can be inserted between the beds as the knitting progresses.

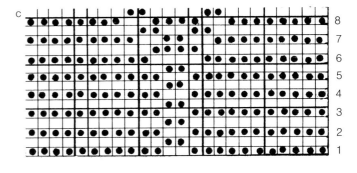

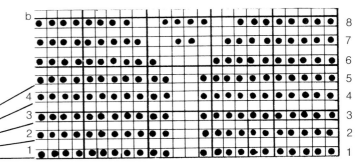

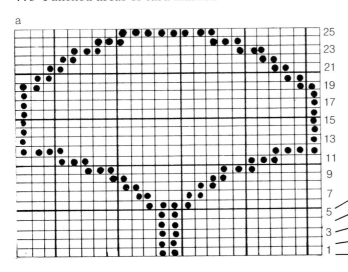

Patterncard definition

The patterncards used for quilted jacquard are identical to those for lined jacquard. The initial design should be predominantly blank with the markings outlining simple geometric shapes.

Knitting method

Quilted and lined jacquard differ only in the tension which is used. The main bed tension is set as high as possible, without the stitches lifting off the needles, to achieve a fabric with a plain backing and a crinkled faceside (figure 78).

Designing patterncards for quilted jacquard

Follow the instructions for designing lined jacquard patterncards bearing in mind that if the pockets are to be filled the outline shape must be very simple.

78 Knitted sample of quilted jacquard

Blister stitch

Blister stitch is a further extension of the above fabrics. Similar methods are used to knit it but the pattern design can be more detailed. The best results are obtained when the larger areas are blistered. This reduces the length and number of floats enclosed in the fabric. The patterncard in figure 20 is suitable for use as a blister fabric. The design was developed on paper but, as indicated in chapter 2, it must be knitted to prove that it works. Displaying the pattern repeats on the PPD does help but it cannot indicate the surface texturing.

The converted patterncard whilst retaining the essence of the original pattern shape has lost the impact of the connecting lines. To keep the pattern within the twenty four stitch discipline is not too difficult but it masks the fact that there is no restriction on the number of rows which can be used. The addition of extra rows allows for the extension of the connecting lines to produce a design even closer to the original.

When the corrected design is knitted as a blister fabric another design fault emerges (figure 79).

79a Knitted sample of blister stitch

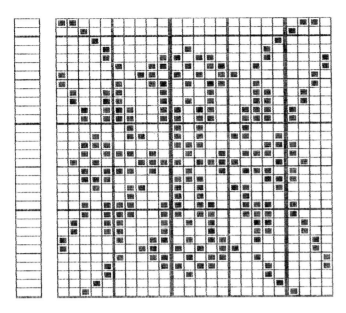

79b Patterncard. Knitting instructions see text

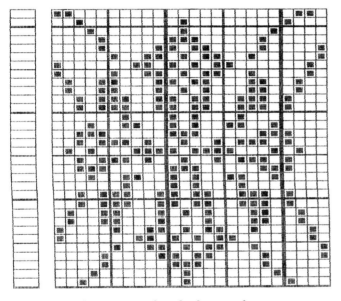

80 Perfected patterncard with elongated pattern shapes. (Needs adapting for use on punchcard machines)

Knitting instructions
see text

The extra rows added to the design force the original shapes even further apart. This creates a section of surface blister sixteen rows deep which obscures the shape which is the main feature of the design. The answer? Elongate the main shape to reduce the blistering. Figure 80 shows the final patterncard.

Fabric definition

Blister stitch is a double thickness, two-colour fabric with a crumpled face side and a single-colour backing. Either the blank or the marked areas of the patterncard can be blistered depending on the way the ribber is set. The blistered areas are knitted on one bed only, the rest is full needle rib with floats from each blister enclosed in the fabric.

Patterncard definition

The markings on the patterncards used for blister stitch are identical to those for lined jacquard. The patterncard in figure 20 is improved if the punched and unpunched areas are arranged in a connecting pattern rather than in isolated shapes (figure 80).

Knitting method

Each colour is knitted separately in two row sequences. Quilted jacquard requires a loose tension on the main carriage to produce a wrinkled surface on the faceside of the fabric. To create blistering on the faceside more rows must be knitted on the main bed than on the ribber. To achieve this the machine is set to elongation and the ribber is disconnected on certain rows. This disconnection creates floats which are contained within the fabric. They are carried across the knitting from one blister to another just as in single-bed Fair Isle.

Electronic machines
Select the type of patterncard and the knitting method required (see *Lined jacquard*, page 90).

Note Mylar sheets for the Knitmaster 500 or 560 machines must be double marked.

1 Knit 1 row, from left to right, with the background yarn to set the memory.

2 Knit 1 row, from right to left, in the background yarn with the main carriage set to slip both ways. The ribber carriage is set to slip both ways.

3 Knit 2 rows in contrast yarn with the main carriage set to slip both ways. The ribber carriage is set with the left button on slip, right button to knit.

4 Knit 2 rows in background yarn with the main carriage set to slip both ways. The ribber carriage is set to slip both ways.

Repeat steps 3 and 4 for the length of the pattern. The tension for the main bed should be as loose as possible without the stitches lifting off the needles.

Punchcard machines

Prepare a patterncard with the same markings as for lined jacquard. The machine must be set to elongation unless the patterncard is marked out in full.

1 Cast on in background yarn, knit a few rows. With the carriage on the right knit one row from right to left to select the first row.

2 Knit two rows in the background yarn with the carriage set to slip both ways and the ribber set to slip both ways.

3 Change to the contrast yarn. Knit 2 rows with the main carriage set to slip and the ribber carriage set with the left button on slip, right button to knit.

4 Change to the background yarn. Knit two rows with the carriage set to slip and the ribber set to slip both ways.

Repeat steps 3 and 4 for the length of the pattern. The tension for the main bed should be as loose as possible without the stitches lifting off the needles.

Slip

With specially adapted patterncards it is possible to produce a fabric with more than two colours in a row. Each colour is knitted independently in two row sequences similar to double jacquard. However, because of the extra movements of the carriages there are limits to the number of colours which can be used. The duomatics with their system of strippers can accommodate up to four colours without any problem; eight movements of the lock produces two rows of actual knitting. The limit for Japanese machines is three colours; six movements of the carriage produces two rows of knitting (figure 81).

Fabric definition

A multicoloured fabric knitted with a ribbing attachment is double sided and has a pattern with three or four colours on the faceside. The reverse side can vary from three colour stripes or pintucks to bird's-eye depending on the setting of the ribber carriage. Floats may be enclosed in the fabric if the ribber is set to slip at any time during a sequence.

Patterncard definition and marking

Patterncards for multicoloured double-bed slip stitch bear little resemblance to the design which will be knitted. Each colour is allocated a row to itself on the patterncard which means that the design is spread over three rows. Every three row sequence must have each square marked across the pattern width as in double jacquard.

As the slip setting is used to knit these designs the patterncards for electronic and punchcard machines are identical except for Knitmaster 500/560 machines which require double marking.

Studying the patterncards for three colours in a row reveals that they operate in a similar way to

81 Knitted sample of three colours in a row

those for double jacquard. The patterncard markings are planned to allow the use of more than one colour in a row without distorting the fabric. They enable the individual to select the desired colour where required across the width of the pattern. The blank areas of the patterncard prevent a colour appearing where it is not needed. As the knitting progresses each of the blank areas is selected in turn until all the needles in a sequence have been knitted.

Knitting method

A fabric with three colours in a row can be knitted on a single- or double-bed machine. There are so many floats on the reverse of a single-bed fabric that it is not a practical proposition. However, single-bed working is ideal to test out a design. As the marking for both is identical, the patterncard can be checked out quite quickly.

Each row of the patterncard must be repeated to allow the carriage to return to the left for a yarn change every two rows. This indicates that the initial selection must take place from the right to the left.

1 Cast on the required number of stitches. Knit a few rows in colour 1. Carriage on right. Knit 1 row from right to left to memorize the pattern. Row count 000.

2 Set the machine to elongation, the main carriage to slip both ways and the ribber carriage for the appropriate backing, if applicable. * Knit 2 rows in colour 1. Row count 002.

3 Change to colour 2, knit 2 rows. Row count 004.

4 Change to colour 3, knit 2 rows. Row count 006 *

Continue to knit from * to * for the full length of the patterncard.

Knitting guidelines

Knitting multicoloured fabrics on the double bed is not too difficult if the following guidelines are observed. Assuming that the ribber is set to knit on every row to produce pintucks on the reverse side:

1 The knitting is easier if the patterncard has three colours in every row. This ensures that a regular colour change is maintained.

2 Make sure that the end needle is not selected. Continuous selection produces six rows of knitting at the end of every two row sequence which creates a frilled edge.

3 After the cast on rows, return the row counter to zero to keep track of which colour is to be knitted, eg if the number is divisible by six then colour 1 needs to be knitted. If the remainder, after dividing by six, is two then colour 2 is the next colour. A remainder of four requires the selection of colour 3.

4 The work must be well and evenly weighted. Move the side weights up the work on a regular basis.

5 Do not rush. A steady speed will produce a more regular fabric without snags in the knitting and the correct colour is more likely to be selected.

6 After each colour change check that the yarn is in the feeder and running freely. Keep it clear of the gatepegs on both beds to avoid dropped stitches.

7 The danger rows of a sequence are rows three and four. This is because four rows have been knitted on the ribber bed and the held (slipped) stitches on the main bed are beginning to lift off the needles. As soon as row five is worked the build-up of rows on the ribber is released as colour 3 slides into its allotted space in the design. Row six completes the sequence and the ridge slips down between the beds ready to begin again.

Designing patterncards for multicoloured double-bed slip

There are two methods of designing patterncards for multicoloured slip stitch.

1 Adapt a Fair Isle card.

2 Design from source.

Each requires a patternchart from which to work. In the case of method 1 the chart is already prepared. Method 2 requires the creation of a design chart. The transfer of these designs to patterncards is identical.

Adapting a Fair Isle patternchart to a three-colours-in-a-row patterncard

1 Select a Fair Isle pattern preferably no more than ten rows deep which has an enclosed shape. A pattern of this depth will require thirty rows of marking if elongation is to be used; sixty rows of marking would be needed if elongation is not available (figure 82a).

2 Shade in the centre of the enclosed shape to give three colours (figure 82b).

3 Mark a blank grid into three row sections numbering each section (figure 82c).

4 Mark each row of each section with the appropriate colour. Check that every stitch in each three row section is marked to avoid mistakes when knitting (figure 82c).

5 Mark the appropriate patterncard into three row sections and afterwards transfer the prepared grid.

Designing a multicoloured patterncard from source

Follow the instructions for creating Fair Isle designs in chapter 2 bearing in mind that

1 The design should not be more than ten rows deep.

2 The pattern should have enclosed shapes.

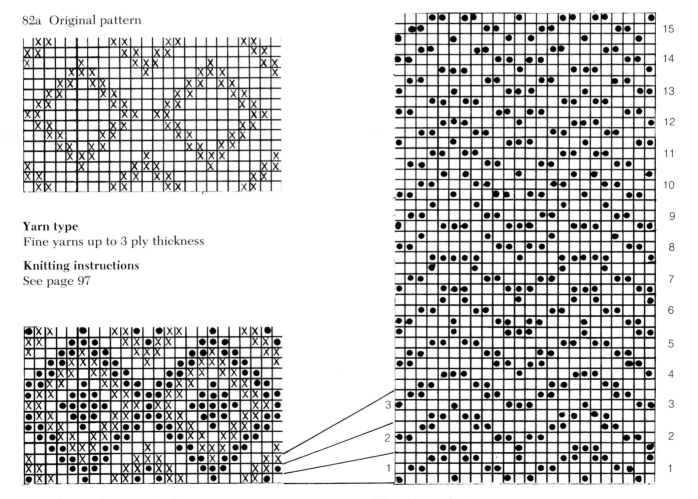

82a Original pattern

Yarn type
Fine yarns up to 3 ply thickness

Knitting instructions
See page 97

82b Three colours marked

82c Patternchart

When the design has been perfected follow the instructions for *Adapting a Fair Isle patternchart to a three-colours-in-a-row patterncard* as above.

Ripple stitch

A ripple stitch fabric is produced by working pintucks on the faceside of the knitting. The pintucks which form when knitting three colours in a row are non-selective. They are worked across all of the needles in work on the ribber bed. Because the pintucks for ripple stitch are worked on the main bed of the machine they can be selected by patterncard to emphasize a pattern feature.

The method of knitting ripple stitch is similar to that for blister stitch. The raised sections of the fabric have an undulating surface rather than a blister to prevent a muddle when knitting

numerous rows over the same needles on one bed only (figure 83).

Fabric definition

A ripple stitch fabric has a full-needle rib background with raised sections, usually in another colour, knitted on one bed only. There are floats from one ripple to another which are enclosed in the fabric. The raised sections knitted on a Japanese machine are usually no more than six rows deep to prevent the stitches from lifting off the needle and causing a muddle.

Patterncard definition

A patterncard for ripple stitch has more areas punched than blank. The blank areas should be no more than three stitches across as they form the floats which will be enclosed in the fabric (figure 84).

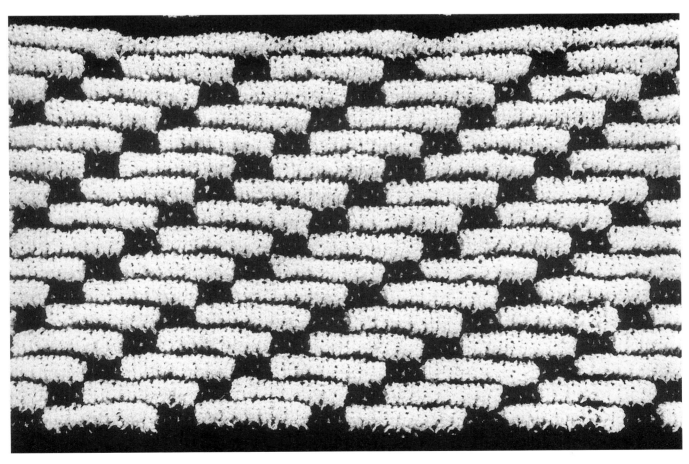

83 Knitted sample of ripple stitch

84a Original design with four pattern repeats
84b First pattern repeat

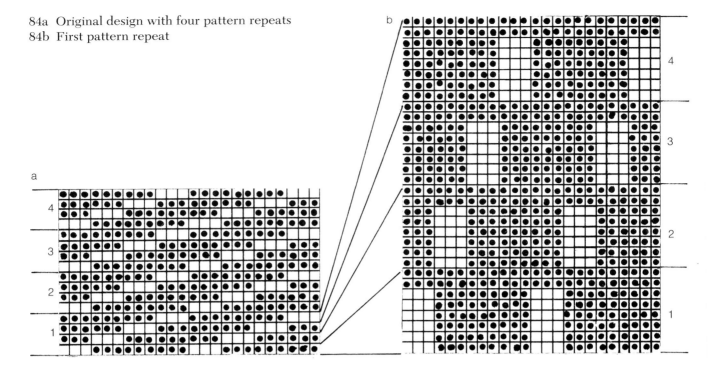

Designing ripple stitch patterncards

There are two methods of designing.

1 Adapt a commercial card.

2 Create a new design.

Whichever method is used it is essential to have a patternchart from which to work. There are no rigid rules to follow in the creation of these patterncards except that best results are obtained by observing the guidelines listed below.

Guidelines

1 Select or create a pattern with a simple outline (figure 84a). The fabric is highly textured and needs clean sharp lines to show this off.

2 Make sure that the selected or created pattern does not have too many rows; six rows are marked for each ripple plus two rows to release the pintucks making eight rows for every row of the patterncard.

3 Avoid designs with large blank areas. Blank areas on a patterncard form long floats in the fabric unless the knitting is reversed, i.e. the blank areas are knitted in ripple stitch.

Converting a design to a ripple stitch patterncard

1 Mark off a blank grid into eight row sections. Number each one.

2 Mark, on the first row of the grid, the areas from the first row of the patterncard which are to form a ripple (figure 84b).

3 Repeat these markings for a further five rows (six rows in all).

4 Mark the last two rows of the first section across the full width of the patterncard (figure 84b).

Repeat for the next and every following row of the chosen design.

Tuck stitch

The addition of a ribber to a knitting machine increases its potential in many ways. Using the ribber in conjunction with tuck stitch can produce textured fabrics with many variations.

Full needle rib

Fabric definition

A fabric knitted with all needles in work on both beds produces double fabric with distorted ribs forming a pattern across the surface of the knitting on the ribber side of the fabric where the tucking occurs (figure 85).

Patterncard definition

As for basic tuck stitch.

Knitting method

1 Requires a fine industrial yarn to produce a viable fabric.

2 All needles in work on both beds.

3 The ribber is set to half pitch.

4 The main carriage is set to tuck throughout. The ribber is set to knit every row.

Designing patterncards

Use the basic tuck cards.

Tuck rib

Tuck ribs are an extension of full needle rib. The texturing on the surface is created by the removal of selected stitches from the main bed to the ribber bed. They can be knitted using the basic patterncards. The same principles used for tuck lace can be applied to tuck rib but instead of leaving needles out of work the stitches are transferred to the ribber. When selected stitches are transferred to the ribber, and needles on the ribber are left in rest position, a new dimension is added to the fabric. The basic tuck cards can be used (figure 86) but special patterncards designed to create a textured fabric with an 'Aran look' will make the fabric more interesting.

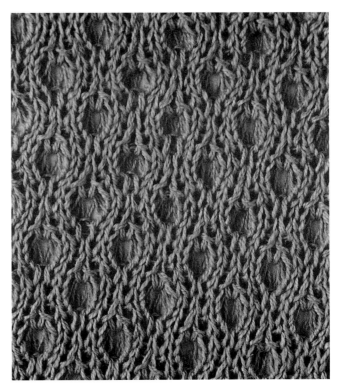

85 Full needle tuck rib

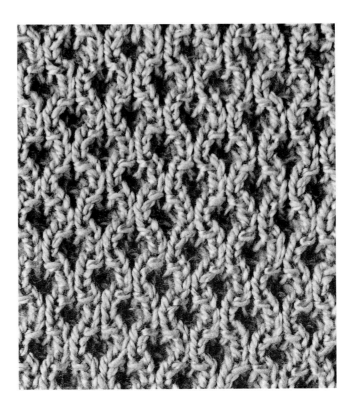

86 Full needle tuck rib with needles transferred to the ribber

Fabric definition

A tuck rib fabric has three different surface textures.

1 Purl stitches.

2 Tuck stitches.

3 Knitted stitches. The knitted stitches can be arranged in various ways.

    a To outline the individual tucked stitches.
    b To form ridges between each geometric tuck section.

Knitting method

1 Selected needles on both beds are in use.

2 The ribber may be on full or half pitch depending on the thickness of yarn and the type of rib being knitted.

3 The main bed is set to tuck and the ribber is set to knit normally throughout.

4 The fabric must be weighted to prevent the knitting from lifting off the needles. However, if too much weight is applied the texturing of the fabric is reduced.

Note The duomatic is renowned for its tuck ribs and for years was the envy of those with Japanese machines. The weightless method of knitting produces the most beautiful 'crunch' to the fabric. The tuck ribs produced on the Japanese machines are clearly not as defined as those produced on the duomatic but they are a good substitute.

Designing tuck rib patterncards

Basic tuck cards can be used to good effect if simple tuck ribs are required. As with all stitch settings there are basic patterns which can be used to build up a library. It may be useful to return to the experiments used for tuck lace. Instead of leaving needles out of work, transfer them to the ribber bed. The effects can be quite surprising.

Card 3 is recognized as being one of the most versatile patterncards around. When used with a 1 × 1 needle arrangement it produces the classic

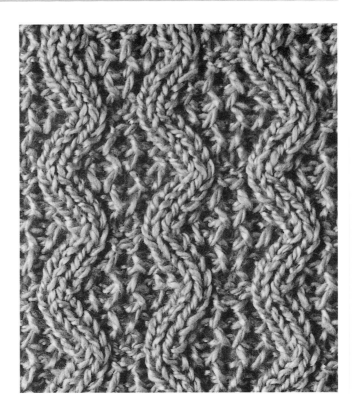

87b Knitted sample

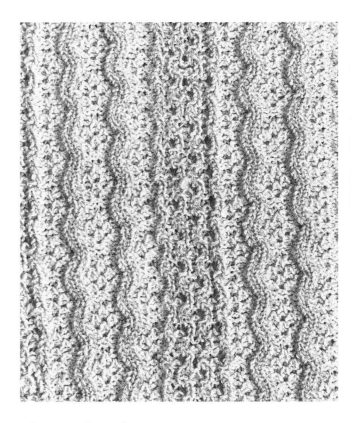

88b Knitted panel

honeycomb pattern (figure 86). Different needle arrangements will produce other patterns. Try them and see.

In figure 43 a patterncard with alternating diamonds was designed. If this is adapted it can be used for tuck rib. The diamonds must be reduced in size to allow for areas of plain knitting between the tuck sections (figure 87a). The stitches which fall between the tuck sections are the ones to be transferred to the ribber. They form wavy ridges on the purlside of the fabric (figure 87b).

These two fabrics are most interesting and should be used as a guide to developing patterncards useful for tuck ribs. A more advanced type of tuck rib has evolved.

Mock Aran

Elsie Smith of Darlington is the person credited with the original fabrics now called 'mock Aran'. They were knitted on the duomatic to begin with, using the pushers and arrow keys. Owners of Japanese machines began to experiment and they produced a very good substitute.

Most knitters have only twenty four stitches available for their patterning base and mock Aran is knitted in panels which change as they spread from the centre of the needlebed. Experiment with lots of different needle selections to see what evolves.

The two tuck rib fabrics can be combined. The *Card 3* tuck pattern must be placed at either side of the diamonds as the pattern is to be used across the width of the garment.

The resulting patterncard in figure 88a is twenty four stitches wide. The fabric panel in figure 88b uses an alteration to the needle arrangement to provide the differences across the panel (figure 89).

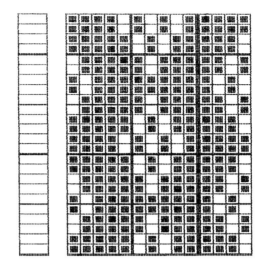

87a Patterncard for reduced diamonds

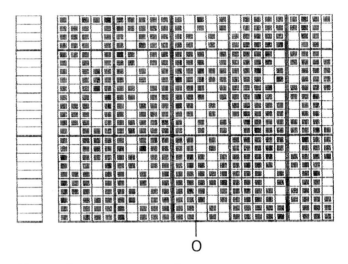

88a Mock Aran patterncard

There are many more mock Aran patterns to be created. The best way to design the patterncards and explore the different needle arrangements is to start as suggested at the beginning of this section. Work through the basic patterncards varying the needle setting and record the results.

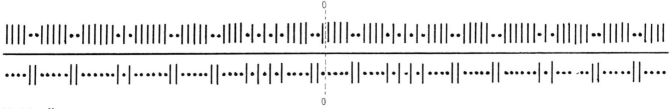

89 Needle arrangement

Garter stitch

The electronic garter carriage is only available for the Brother machines. Its introduction has widened the scope of stitch structures which can be knitted. Although the attachment has opened up a new source of patterning for the machine knitter it does have its disadvantages.

1 Only one colour can be knitted at a time.

2 It is quite slow.

3 It ties up a machine for prolonged lengths of time.

However, the advantages do outweigh the disadvantages for those who own more than one knitting machine.

1 The garter carriage can be left to knit without the operator present.

2 It can cast on and off automatically when the operator is present.

3 It produces a fabric previously unavailable to machine knitters.

Until this new development, garter stitch was confined to hand knitting. The garter bar enabled whole rows to be knitted in garter stitch but detailed patterns required hand tooling. The garter carriage should be purchased in addition to a ribbing attachment rather than as a replacement.

Fabric definition

A garter stitch fabric is of single thickness with both knit and purl stitches on the face and reverse side. Where a knit stitch appears on the faceside a purl stitch is produced on the reverse of the fabric and vice versa.

Fabric comparison

The fabric proportions depend entirely on the type of patterncard being used. A fabric knitted with vertical ribs will be longer and narrower than one with horizontal ridges even though the same number of stitches and rows are used (figure 90).

90a Ridges (14sts 32 rows)

90b Ribs (32sts 22 rows)

Knitting method

Garter stitch fabric is knitted automatically, independent of an operator, on the single-bed machine. To set up, see the manual.

The blank areas of the patterncard are knitted with the main bed needles to produce a purl stitch on the side of the fabric which faces the knitter.

The punched/marked areas of the patterncard are knitted with the garter carriage needle to produce a knit stitch on the side of the fabric which faces the knitter.

Patterncard definition

Most commercial patterncards for garter stitch have large unmarked areas with pattern outlines similar to Fair Isle. Some can be too bitty.

A balance of punched and unpunched areas produces pleasing results. Where the areas of punched, unpunched and mixed areas of marking are arranged over the patterncard in separate defined shapes the results can be spectacular.

The blank areas of a patterncard produce a purl stitch on the surface of the knitting as it faces the knitter.

The punched/marked areas of the card produce a knit stitch on the surface of the knitting which faces the knitter.

Basic garter stitch patterns

As with the other stitches there are pattern arrangements which form the basis of design (figure 91). When knitted

1 Blank areas produce purl stitches on the side of the fabric which faces the knitter.

2 Punched/marked areas produce knit stitches on the side which faces the knitter.

3 Vertical strips produce ribs. The width of each rib depends on the number of stitches in each stripe.

4 Horizontal stripes produce ridges in the fabric. The depth of ridge depends on the number of rows in the stripes.

5 Punching every alternate square produces moss stitch.

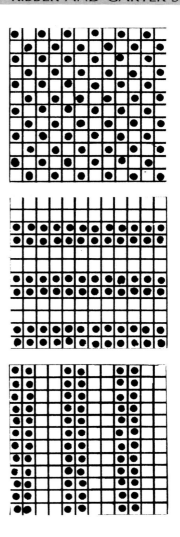

91 Basic patterncards for garter stitch

Creating garter stitch patterncards

There are numerous patterncards already available which can be used with the garter carriage. Select those which have strong pattern features. Patterncards designated for Fair Isle, release stitch and punch lace produce the most striking fabrics.

Types of pattern

1 A small pattern in the background with an outline shape in knit stitch with an enclosed shape in purl stitch.

2 A small pattern in the background with an outline shape in purl stitch with an enclosed shape in knit stitch.

3 Combinations of rib stitch and garter stitch.

4 Combinations of rib, garter and moss stitch.

The first two pattern types can be sketched to help with the designing. The second two can also be sketched but the distortion of the rib and garter stitch ridges in the fabric when the design is knitted will not be indicated. The sample in figure 92, pattern 419 from *Stitch World* is an example of a fabric combining sections of knitting, purling, ribbing and moss stitch.

Ribbed pleats

As discussed previously, true pleats with sections of double fabric can only be knitted on machines with a ribbing attachment. However, a variety of ribbed pleats can be knitted with the garter carriage. There are different categories of pleats, each has numerous variations.

1 Ribbed.

2 Accordion.

3 Knife pleats.

The electronic machines allow a more flexible approach to the development of these pleat effects as any pattern width can be used. However, the twenty four stitch discipline has served very well for years and is a challenge to the designer's ingenuity.

Rib effects

The standard ribbed welts can be knitted using the garter carriage and a patterncard. The results are very similar to hand knitted ribs. More interesting are the rib arrangements which look like pleats.

When knitting ordinary ribs, by hand or machine, the purl stitches recede, the knit stitches advance. Wider rib arrangements emphasize this fact (figure 93). The sample of fabric in figure 93a was knitted using five knit stitches and four purl stitches across the needle bed. Originally this setting was knitted using a ribber on half pitch. The half pitch setting creates an overlap of stitches where the gauge is reduced. This helps to

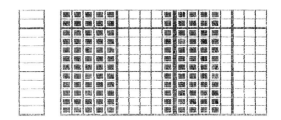

94a 5 × 4

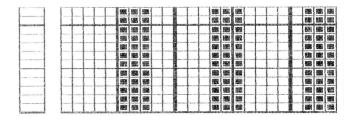

94b 5 × 3

94 Patterncards for rib and roll pleats

pull the fabric into the characteristic curves. It is not possible to reduce the gauge when using the garter carriage but a similar effect is achieved using the patterncard in figure 94.

Many rib arrangements are possible within the twenty four stitch discipline. Obviously a 5 × 4 pattern will not fit and adjustments must be made (figure 94b). Owners of electronic machines are not restricted by pattern bases, which eases the design process. Only one row of a patterncard need be marked for electronic machines.

Most wide ribbed pleats have a rounded look to them. The addition of a section of knitting which will lie flat should produce a fabric which looks more like conventional pleats.

The standard 1 × 1 rib arrangement is ideal for the flat section. It is a firm flat fabric, slightly heavier than the other sections and it remains rigid as the knit and purl stitches fall into their natural shapes.

Creating rib and roll pleats

Use a twelve stitch base to keep the pleats within the twenty four stitch pattern discipline.

A rib of three knit stitches and five purl stitches leaves four stitches spare. These four stitches leave room for alternating marks on the patterncard (figure 95).

92 Knitted sample using Brother pattern 419 from *Stitch World*

93a 5 stitches marked

93b 5 stitches blank

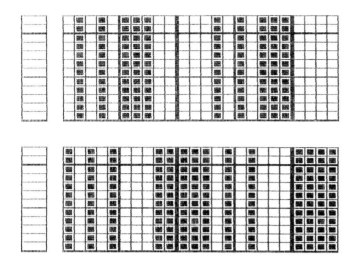

95 Patterncard for rib and roll pleats with 1 × 1 section

Before knitting the pleats mark out the arrangement on paper. Draw a line in between the marks and blanks to illustrate the way the pleat should fall when released from the machine (figure 96). It is not possible to reproduce the full effect of the pleat when using an illustration but a clear indication of what will happen is shown. When the knitting is released from the machine the fabric contracts and forms a pleated fabric which measures only a fraction of the width of the original.

The patterncard illustrated is a simple example of developing a pleat which can be easily knitted on the garter carriage. If a wider pleat is required and only twenty four stitches are available the patterncard has twelve stitches spare which can be utilized as desired.

Despite the apparent slowness of the garter carriage it does not take long for a sample sixty

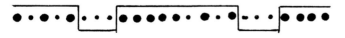

96a 5 stitches marked

96b 3 stitches marked

96 Diagram of rib and roll pleats

stitches wide and fifty rows in length to be knitted. However, if you cannot wait for a few minutes to see the result then use the diagram method suggested above. The paper method illustrates, immediately, the direction in which the pleats will face.

The variations on rib and roll pleats are too numerous to mention. Experiment on paper or use the garter carriage and see how many variations you can create.

Accordion pleats

Accordion pleats vary in depth according to the number of stitches in each pleat. Pilsener pleating, an example of accordion pleats, is based on the old Triangular stitch from Scotland (figure 97). Triangular stitch is sometimes called 'mock kilting' because of its tendency to roll up into pleats. The pilsener pleats featured in Barbara Walker's *A Second Treasury of Knitting Patterns* have openwork edging each triangle. As open work is not possible using the garter carriage the pattern needs to be altered to suit the machine.

The pilsener pleating in figure 97 is an adaptation of a stitch used in a garment from the Rachel Kay Shuttleworth collection at Gawthorpe Hall, Padiham, Lancashire. The larger version is ideal for adults but unless using very fine yarn it forms pleats which are too deep for small garments. The adapted version has exactly the same properties but is on a smaller scale much more suited for use in children's garments (figure 98).

Barbara Walker suggests leaving the fabric unpressed to encourage the pleats to form. This is not the ideal way to deal with fabric as its nature can alter when washed, particularly if a natural fibre has been used. Modern methods of treating fabric have shown that a steam press is all that is required to set the fabric and retain its natural texture. Other types of ribbed pleating can be created if the relationship between the machine, the patterncard and the fabric can be understood. Analyzing the pilsener pleats in figure 97 and 98 may help.

1 The unpunched vertical lines form a purl stitch which moves to the back of the knitting.

97a Knitted sample: Pilsener pleats – original size

98a Knitted sample: Pilsener pleats – larger size

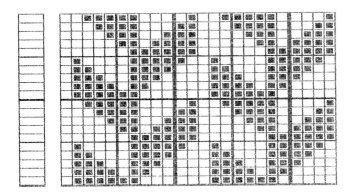

97b Patterncard

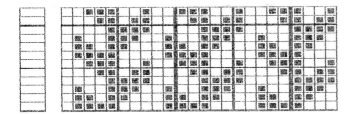

98b Patterncard

2 The vertical punched/marked lines form a knit stitch which moves to the front of the knitting.

3 The alternating parallelograms of knit and purl stitches push the vertical lines of the patterncard into a wavy line on the knitting.

By definition – assuming that the side of the fabric facing the knitter when it is on the machine is to be used as the rightside

1 where a surface fold is needed on a pleat, a marked square is needed on the patterncard (figure 99)

2 where a backwards fold is required on a pleat, the square is left blank (figure 99).

The above information can be used to design any number of accordion pleats with varying depths. The information can also be utilized to design knife pleats.

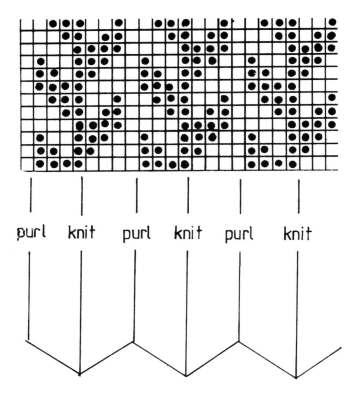

purl   knit   purl   knit   purl   knit

99 Accordion pleats – illustrating the relationship of the patterncard marking to the direction of the pleat

100 Knife pleat

Knife pleats

When analyzing the fabric in figures 97 and 98 it was noted that a marked square is needed for the outward facing fold and an unmarked square is needed for the inner fold. The width of each pleat and the amount of overlap can vary depending on the type of machine being used (figure 100).

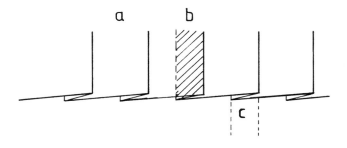

101 Diagram of pleat
a Section visible all the time
b Fold back section
c Section hidden underneath the fold back

There are three sections to a knife pleat.

a The first section is the one which is on view all the time, section a (figure 101).
b The second section is the one which folds back underneath this surface and is very rarely seen, section b (figure 101).
c The third section is the layer of fabric behind the foldover which is seen as the pleats fall open when the garment is worn, section c (figure 101).

Section (a) and section (c) are connected. They can have separate patterns or a continuing one across the surface of the pleat. The decision is the designer's.

Designing patterncards for knife pleats

1 Draw a diagram of a knife pleat on plain paper indicating the amount of overlap required (figure 102a).

2 Mark in the number of stitches required for each section. Pay particular attention if the pattern base is twenty four stitches (figure 102a).

3 Open out the 'pleats' and mark them on a grid over the correct number of stitches noting the direction of the fold. Each square represents one stitch (figure 102b).

4 Mark on the grid where a knit stitch is required for the outer pleat fold (figure 102c).

5 Leave the inner fold line unmarked.

6 Fill in the remaining sections (figure 102c).

7 Transfer these marks to the appropriate patterncard (figure 102d).

As a general rule the rib and roll pleats only require a single row of marking on electronic machines. Accordion pleats and knife pleats with a surface pattern will need to be marked in full. Owners of punchcard machines must ensure that there is sufficient marking to allow the card to rotate.

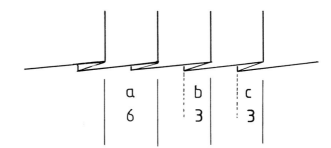

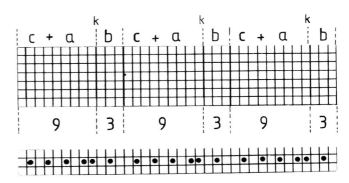

102a Diagram of pleat with stiches marked (top)
102b Pleats opened out (centre)
102c Diagram of patterncard. Repeat vertically (bottom)

7 BRAIDS AND EDGINGS

Knitted braids and edgings allow the knitter to produce decorative trims which match and blend with the knitted item in a way which is not possible when buying commercial trimmings. Some are more difficult to design than others but all are worth the effort. There are many types which range through all the stitch settings. Details of how to design some of these are given below.

Fair Isle

Any small Fair Isle pattern can be used as an edging or binding. A double band knitted in Fair Isle could prove to be too thick. To eliminate one layer of yarn use the single motif setting on the side of the band which will be on the outside of the garment.

Slip stitch

Once the principle of designing petal slip stitch and its variations has been understood, i.e. blank areas of the patterncard will disappear when knitted, it becomes clear that the same rules can be applied to braids and edgings.

Flower braids (figure 103)

Flower braids are simple to design and knit and are extremely versatile. The background and flower yarns are knitted separately. The only connection the petal yarn has with the background is on the rows where the colour is changed. This enables the braid to be knitted without floats except where the flowers change colour.

Designing flower braids

1 Sketch the type of flower required, i.e. four, five or six petals (figure 104a).

2 Mark where the slip sections on the sketch occur as explained in chapter 3 page 41 (figure 104b).

3 Decide the width of the petal required. This will determine the number of rows in each petal.

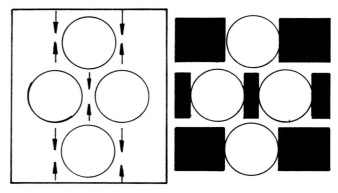

104 Developing a patterncard for flower braids
104a Original idea with arrows to indicate the collection of the fabric (left)
104b Slip blocks marked (right)

103 Flower braid

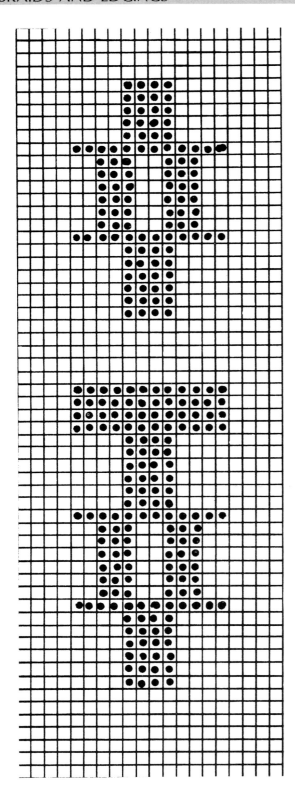

Preparing a working chart

1 Mark the areas from figure 104b which will knit (figure 105a). The proportion of the grid is immaterial as the working chart does not represent how the design will look when it is knitted.

2 Decide how many rows are needed between each flower. Mark them on the chart (figure 105b).

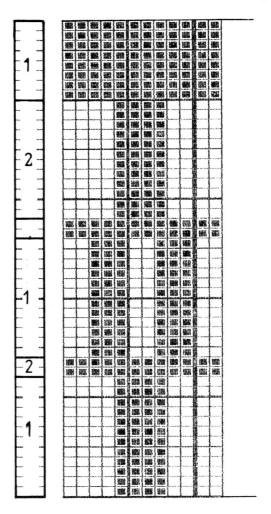

105c Double marked patterncard for flower braid

Yarn type
Colour 1 Any thickness up to 4 ply
Colour 2 Select a yarn slightly thinner than colour

Knitting instructions
1 Cast on the required number of stitches
2 Knit 4 rows in colour 2
3 Set the machine and carriage as appropriate
4 Knit in slip stitch throughout, changing the yarn as
   indicated

105 Converting a design to a patterncard
105a Knit sections marked (top)
105b Chart of patterncard (below)

Converting a working chart to a patterncard

Duomatics

1 Transfer the slip blocks to the patterncard as they appear in figure 105b. Leave blank rows between the rows of petals and between each flower for the stocking stitch rows.

2 Repeat vertically until the pattern card is long enough to rotate.

3 Make sure that the designs are those which can be elongated.

Electronic machines

There are two methods available to electronic owners.

Method 1 Transfer the chart as in step 1 for the duomatic and use the negative button to reverse the reading when knitting.

Method 2 Mark the areas which are to knit remembering the stocking stitch rows between the petals and each flower. Only one repeat is necessary.

Punchcard machines

1 Follow the instructions for method 2 on the electronic.

2 Repeat the design vertically until the card is long enough to rotate.

The completed patterncard is shown in figure 105c.

Guidelines to designing flower braids

1 An even number of rows must separate each flower.

2 The number of rows which separate each flower determines their spacing.

3 The number of stitches in the petals determines the number of rows to be knitted, i.e. two stitches in each petal – up to eight rows, three stitches in each petal – up to twelve rows.

4 The type of yarn used determines the size of the flower.

5 The number of stitches across the braid determines its width.

Knitting method

The braids are knitted using the slip setting throughout. There are virtually no floats. If using a colour changer make sure that the background yarn is on the left of all the other yarns. This avoids floats on the back of the braid and prevents the yarn from snarling.

Variations

The same patterncard can be varied in a number of ways.

1 The flowers can be:

    a the same colour
    b all different colours
    c a sequence of colours
    d knitted in thin yarn
    e knitted in thick yarn.

2 The background can be:

    a knitted in thick yarn
    b knitted in thin yarn.

Each of the adaptations to the flower can be used in conjunction with a thick or thin yarn. Each combination will produce a different result.

Looped braids (figure 106)

Looped braids using the slip setting can be produced automatically by patterncard on Japanese electronic and punchcard machines provided the pattern is no wider than that available on the chosen knitting machine. They are knitted in one colour and, because of the way the patterncard is designed, there are no floats.

Note Owners of duomatic machines are not able to knit these braids automatically because of the deco selection system. They can be knitted using manual selection.

106a Looped braids

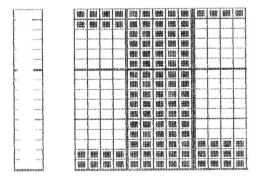

106b Patterncard

Planning a looped braid

It is difficult to visualize the braid which will be
produced by a particular pattern. They are
planned on the card in such a way as to eliminate
the strands of yarn across the work (figure 106). It
is necessary to isolate the stitches which will form
the loop and to knit on these for the desired
number of rows.

If knitting on the centre five stitches of an
eleven stitch braid then three stitches each side of
the centre group must be placed in normal
working position (figure 107). The machine is
using the slip setting. Any needles in normal
working position will be bypassed by the carriage
for the desired number of rows.

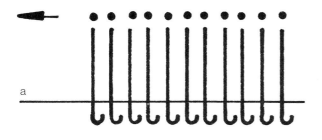

a

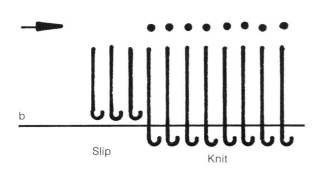

b

Slip   Knit

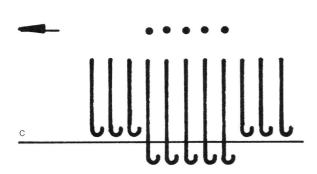

c

Direction of carriage

Patterncard marking

107 Needle selection for looped braids
107a All needles selected
107b Three needles in slip position
107c Two groups of three needles in slip position

For automatic selection of the centre needles

1 The patterncard is left blank over three stitches at one side on row 3 (figure 108a). As the braid is in one colour, either side can be used as the starting point.

2 The pattern card is left blank for three stitches on the second side. This leaves five needles to work on in the centre of the braid (figure 108b).

3 The patterncard is marked over these five needles with the required number of rows (figure 108c).

4 Before the next full width section can be knitted the first set of needles must be returned to upper working position. This is done by marking three stitches on the patterncard at the same side as they were omitted on the first row (figure 108d).

5 On the next row of the patterncard the remaining set of three needles is marked on the patterncard at the opposite side to those in step 4 (figure 108e).

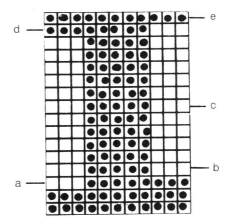

108 Analysis of looped braid patterncard
108a First group of needles to slip
108b Second group of needles to slip
108c Centre five needles in knit position
108d First group of needles returned to knit position
108e Second group of needles returned to knit position

When knitted, this arrangement will return all the needles to upper working position to be repeated for the desired number of rows.

The braid described above is a simple example. Many more complicated braids can be designed using the following guidelines.

Guidelines to designing looped braids

1 The depth of the number of rows which span the full width of the braid must be an even number.

2 The depth of the number of rows which span the full width of the braid must be the same on each side.

3 The number of rows knitted across the full width of the braid determines the size of the loop.

4 The number of rows in a loop determines its length.

5 The number of stitches in a loop determines its width.

109a Self coloured trim with bobbles

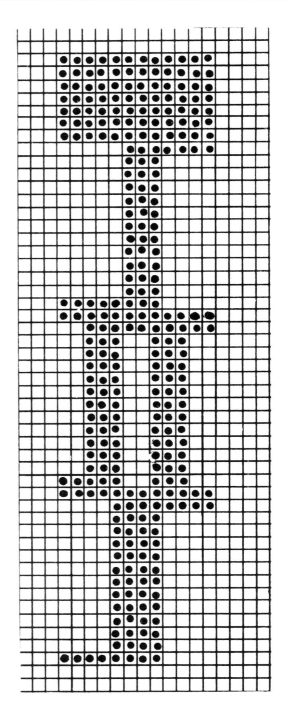

109b Patternchart

Occasionally textured braids in one colour are required. They can be designed using a combination of the above instructions (figure 109).

Flower braids have the background and petal yarn virtually separate. The looped braids are

110 Decorative hems

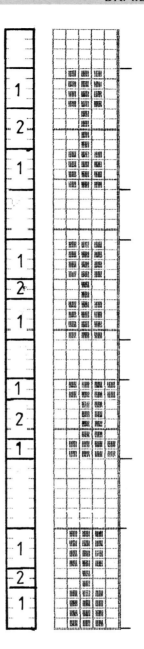

111 Patterncards for two colour hems

Yarn type
Any suitable yarn

Knitting instructions
1 Cast on over required number of rows
2 Knit a plain section of hem
3 Set the carriage and machine to the appropriate stitch
4 Knit in either slip or tuck stitch changing the yarn as indicated on the selected patterncard

arranged on the patterncard in such a way as to eliminate floats (figure 108). By adjusting the flower braid patterncards to return certain needles to working position, in the same way as the looped braids, self coloured trims with bobbles are possible (figure 109).

Decorative hems

Simple two-colour hems are a useful addition to this collection of edgings. They only require one row of a patterncard and can be used with either the tuck or slip setting (figure 110). The more complicated versions with a second colour introduced require a longer patterncard (figure 111).

The hems can be rather bulky depending on the number of rows which are slipped. The slip sections are enclosed in the hem causing some of them to curve. This makes them ideal for trimming armholes and necks.

Tuck stitch

Shell braids

The shell braids which are knitted in tuck stitch, or manually, are widely used (figure 112). The fact that they are still around after many years of use indicates their versatility. The shell braids have a built-in selvedge which makes use of the natural roll on the edge of a knitted fabric.

Because the tuck stitch setting collects loops of yarn in the hooks of the non-selected needles not many rows can be knitted before a muddle occurs. However, the fact that loops of yarn are lifted above the level of the row in which they are knitted causes the fabric to pucker in a very obvious way.

The manuals advise that not more than four rows of tuck stitch be knitted before the loops are released by the patterncard. They also advise that the tuck sections of the patterncard are placed quite close together to avoid large areas of stocking stitch. The extra rows needed to form the tuck effect may cause these plain areas to bubble and detract from the main pattern.

The designer can make use of these guidelines to produce interesting edgings which overrule the generally accepted principles of this stitch setting.

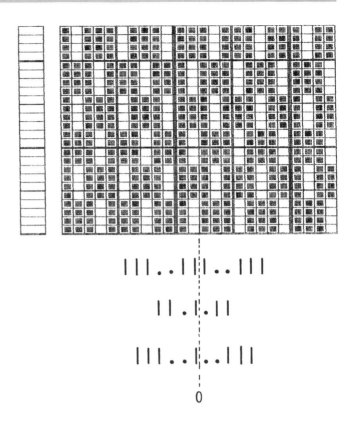

```
I I I . . I I I . . I I I

I I . I . I I

I I I . . I . . I I I

              0
```

112b Patterncard with needle arrangements

1 Knit extra rows to produce a more noticeable tuck in the fabric.

2 Increase the spacing between the tuck patterns to create raised areas of fabric where the plain sections of knitting occur.

It follows therefore that a patterncard can be designed to produce a fabric with areas which bubble in a controlled way. Figure 113a is knitted using a combination of stocking stitch with tuck stitch areas at each side. The tuck areas form a shell edging which rolls over to form a selvedge. The ruched braid/frill in figure 113 is knitted with two needles left out of work. Shirring elastic has been introduced into the centre of figure 113b to emphasize the ruching.

Knitting method

The frill is knitted using tuck stitch throughout. The yarn used in the illustration is extremely fine

112a Shell braids

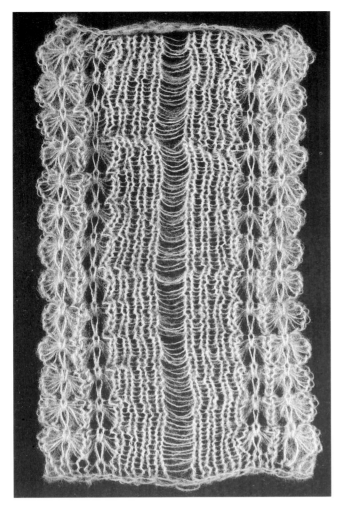

113a Plain

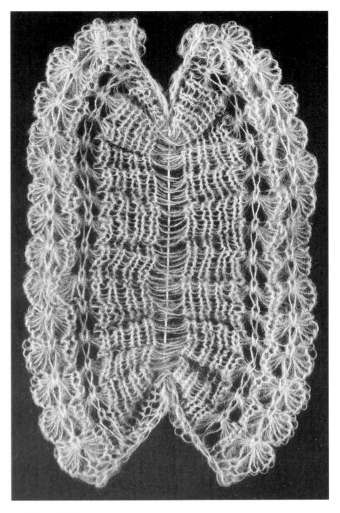

113b with lycra

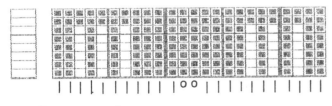

O Empty needles

| Needles in work

113c Patterncard

Yarn type
Yarn of any thickness

Knitting instructions
1 Cast on over needles indicated
2 Set carriage and machine as appropriate
3 Knit in tuck stitch throughout to the required length

and must be evenly weighted. Too much weight will reduce the amount of ruching.

Only a few examples of decorative trims have been included due to lack of space. Many more can be developed from the above ideas and from the ones in common use. It is useful to create a file of as many as possible for future reference.

8 ADVANCED AND MIXED TECHNIQUES

Previous chapters have outlined methods of designing patterncards for different types of stitches. This one will cover ideas for using these patterncards in a different way either by adapting them, combining techniques, altering the colour change sequence or the stitch setting. It is essential to explore the possibilities of any patterncard rather than confine its use to one technique only. Not all of them can be developed successfully but surprising things can emerge when experimenting.

Fair Isle

Changing the yarn texture, reversing the colour scheme and using different thicknesses of yarn are simple ways to add interest to a Fair Isle patterncard. A more advanced technique is to combine Fair Isle and lace on the same patterncard.

Fair Isle and lace

Fabric with a combination of Fair Isle and lace, knitted in separate bands, is often used by designers (figure 114). A more unusual fabric can be produced by combining the two techniques (figure 115). Most lace cards have two blank rows between each lace sequence. These blank (unpunched) rows are the key to creating a lace patterncard with a Fair Isle insert.

Note These fabrics are better knitted on machines which have a lace carriage which is only capable of transfer and selection. Those machines with lace carriages which select, transfer and knit, will knit the patterns but as this means changing from one carriage to another after every few rows it is not really practical.

The instructions for designing Fair Isle pattern cards are given in chapter 2. The lace card markings and their relationship to the carriage movements are explained in chapter 5. By combining this knowledge new fabric designs can be produced.

Designing Fair Isle and lace cards

There are two ways to approach the designing of these cards.

1 Adapt a commercial card.

2 Create an original design.

Adapting commercial cards

1 Select a suitable card from a punchcard pattern book or a pre-punched lace card. Suitable cards, usually simple transfer lace, are those which, when tilted, show an outline shape of lace with an unpunched section clearly defined. The patterncard in figure 116, number 562 from Brother punchcard pattern book 3, is a good example.

114 Fair Isle and lace bands

115 Fair Isle and lace combined

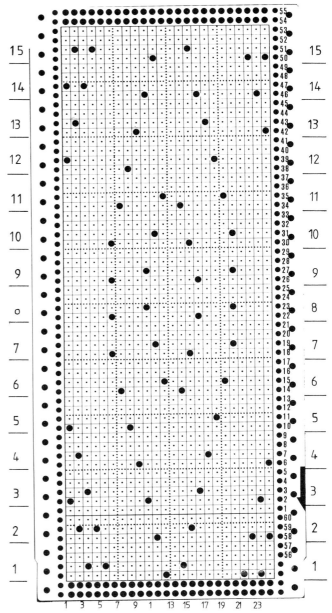

116 Card 562 from *Brother Pattern Book 3* indicating the row sequences of the patterncard

2 Convert the lace design to a lace chart on proportional graph paper as instructed on page 70, leaving one blank row between each pattern sequence (figure 117a). This blank row is where the Fair Isle markings need to be placed.

3 Mark in pencil on the blank row where the contrast colour is required (figure 117b).

4 Mark on the row below where the contrast colour is required (figure 117c).

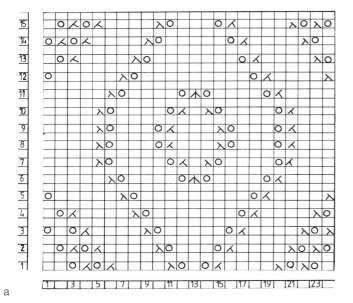

a

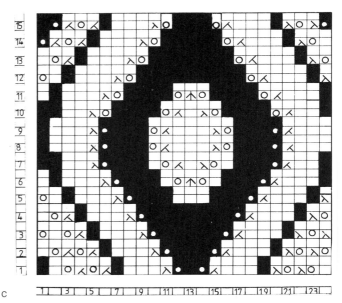

c

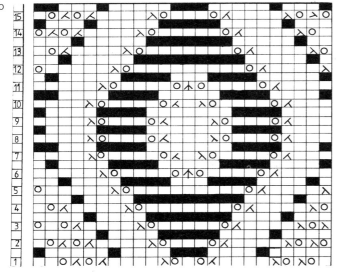

b

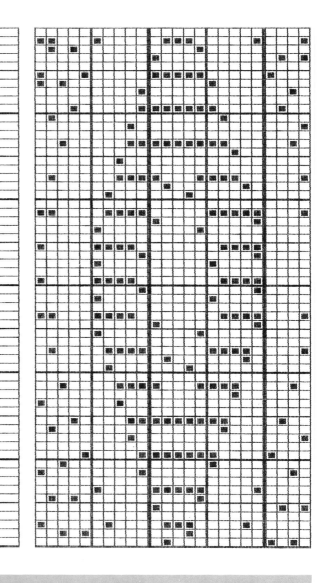

d

117a Lace chart
117b Fair Isle marked
117c Fair Isle marking complete
117d Fair Isle and lace patterncard for Brother
Electronic

Yarn type
Colours 1 and 2 Yarns of a similar thickness

Note If one of the contrast squares has an empty
needle symbol, mark the top section of that square
to indicate that the empty needle is to be knitted
in the contrast colour (figure 117c).

Guidelines to converting Fair Isle and lace patterncharts to patterncards

Because of the way that electronic and punchcard machines interpret the patterncard the patterncard markings for this type of fabric differ between the electronic and the punchcard machines. On the electronic machine the mylar sheet rotates each time a carriage is moved. On a punchcard machine the card only moves on when a carriage changes direction.

Electronic machines

1 The lace sequence is marked as normal, see page 74, chapter 5.

2 The Fair Isle markings are placed on the blank rows which are normally used by the lace carriage to travel to and fro across the needlebed. Both rows must be marked for Fair Isle (figure 117d).

Note The example used in figure 117 is for cards which repeat the same Fair Isle design for two rows. Because the electronic machine moves the mylar sheet every time a carriage is moved the Fair Isle markings can be different on each row. This facility allows greater design possibilities.

Punchcard machines

1 The lace sequence is marked as normal, see page 74.

2 The Fair Isle marking is placed on the *first* blank row after each lace sequence (figure 118).

Note Punchcard machines repeat the Fair Isle row because the punchcard will only rotate when the direction of the carriages is altered.

Knitting method

When knitting normal lace the blank rows are used by the lace carriage to travel across the needlebed. The main carriage is not usually connected to the timing belt, therefore it can be moved as many times as you wish before continuing with the lace pattern. The lace carriage is always connected to the timing belt and therefore the pattern card.

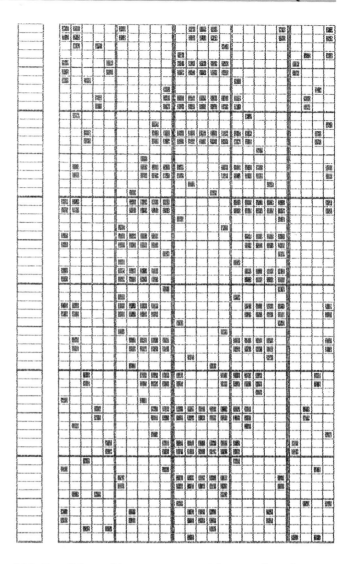

118 Fair Isle and lace patterncard for punchcard machines

Knitting instructions
see page 126

When knitting Fair Isle and lace combination patterns the main carriage is also connected to the timing belt and therefore the patterncard. It is important that only one carriage is on the needlebed at a time otherwise damage can occur. The use of both carriages connected to the timing belt is not recommended by the manufacturers but if you make sure that the first carriage is on the extension rail *before* the second one is moved no harm should come to the machine.

1 The Fair Isle markings are placed on the blank rows which normally allow the lace carriage to

select and transfer stitches and/or return it to its resting place.

2 The Fair Isle markings make it necessary to work from the right with the lace carriage otherwise the lace transfers are in the wrong direction.

3 The main carriage selects the lace pattern needles when it returns to the left. Therefore, to transfer the selected stitches to the left the lace carriage must move from the right to keep the pattern correct.

4 Working with the lace carriage from the right reduces the number of movements; e.g. simple transfer lace, which normally needs four movements of the lace carriage, requires only two movements to complete the sequence.

Knitting instructions

1 Lock the card on row 1, move the lace carriage from left to right, release the card and continue with the lace sequence for two more rows. The lace carriage is on the right. On the last row the needles for the Fair Isle are selected by the lace carriage.

2 The main carriage, set to KC II, is on the left. Select the Fair Isle setting, insert the second colour in feeder B and knit two rows. The second row of the sequence selects the lace needles

3 Knit two rows of lace.

Continue steps 2 and 3 until the pattern is completed.

Creating new patterncards

1 Mark out a lace pattern on a proportional grid as detailed in chapter 5, page 70, leaving one blank row between each lace sequence. Use the new lace patterncard from chapter 5, figure 64.

2 Mark the Fair Isle where appropriate on the blank rows between the lace sequences.

3 Convert the design to a patterncard chart on the grid as detailed previously using the appropriate instructions.

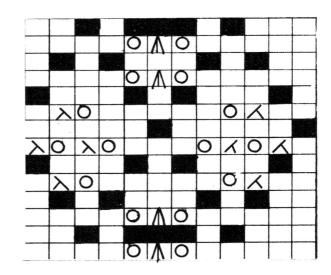

119a Mark the Fair Isle on the lace chart from figure 64

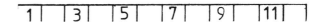

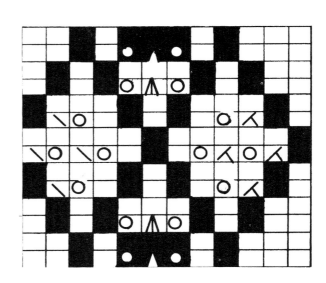

119b Patterncard chart

4 Transfer the patterncard chart onto a punchcard or mylar sheet (figure 119).

Figure 120 illustrates the new Fair Isle and lace pattern. As an understanding of the fabric increases, more intricate designs can be created with ease.

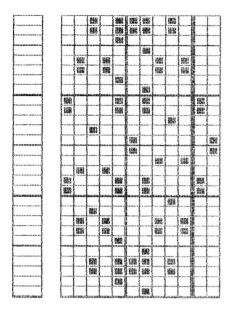

119c Patterncard

Yarn type
Colours 1 and 2 Any yarn suitable for lace

Knitting instructions
See page 126

120 New Fair Isle and lace

Slip stitch

Exploring the ruched patterncard

The ruched patterncard developed in chapter 3 can be given a different look by introducing colour changes. The basic rules of slip stitch are applied.

1 The blank areas of the card will disappear when the card is knitted.

2 The punched sections of the card will be visible when the card is knitted.

Knitting numerous rows which will not be visible on the faceside of the fabric means that new colours can be introduced which will disappear behind the slip bars as dictated by the patterncard. If desired the colour changes can be planned on an empty grid.

Figure 121 is a grid of the patternchart with the slip areas marked. The grid has double marking. Copy it and fill it in with the desired colours. Figure 122 illustrates how to use it. Arrows are drawn onto the grid to show the direction in which the fabric will be pulled when the pattern is knitted. The arrows meet in the centre of the blocks pulling up the coloured sections which disappear behind them to form the shape which will be created when the pattern is knitted. For a more detailed explanation see chapter 3 page 41. Different colour sequences produce fabrics with a totally different look (figure 123).

This method does not indicate the shape of each section but it eases the problem of knowing when to change the colour.

1 The colour of a slip bar is determined by the colour which is marked at the bottom and/or top of a slip block (figure 122).

2 Any colour in contact with the slip blocks across the width of the pattern grid will be hidden by the slip bar (figure 122).

The same patterncard can be used as a single motif to produce braids and edgings (figure 124). Different sections of the patterncard are selected to create the various effects. The needle arrangements illustrated in figure 125 should be used in conjunction with the ruched patterncard.

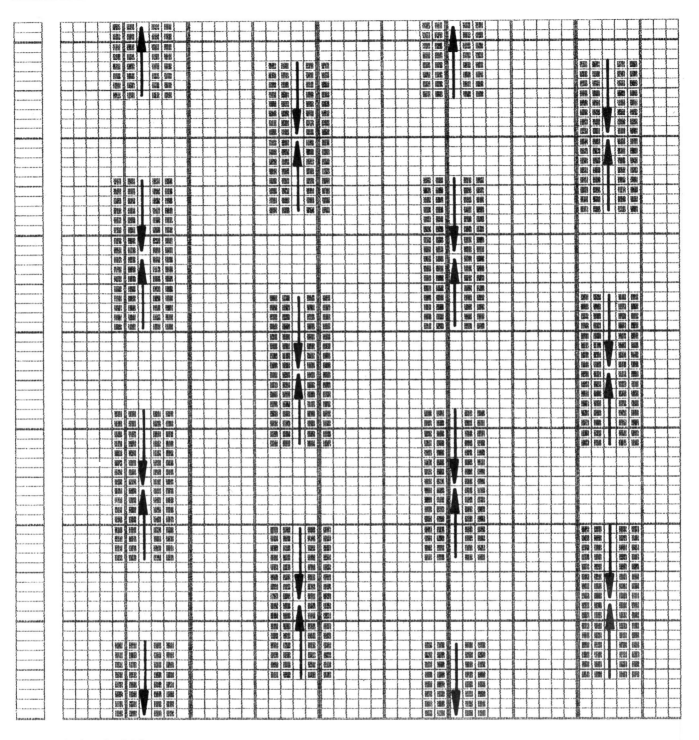

121 Grid of ruched fabric

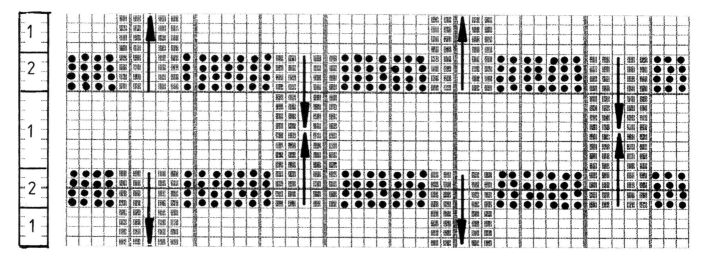

122a (left) Use of grid

123a (below) Changed colour sequence

Yarn type
Colours 1 and 2 Yarns of equal thickness

Knitting instructions
1 Cast on required number of stitches
2 Set carriage and machine as appropriate
3 Knit in slip stitch throughout changing colour as indicated

122b Knitted sample

123b Knitted sample

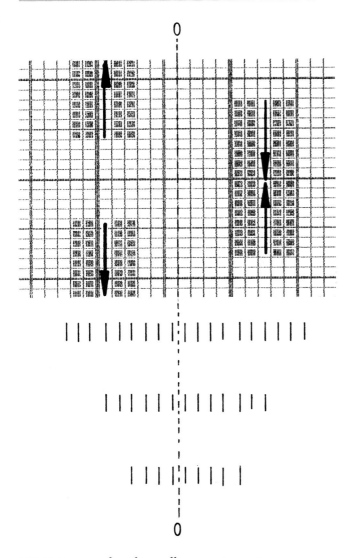

125 Patterncard with needle arrangement

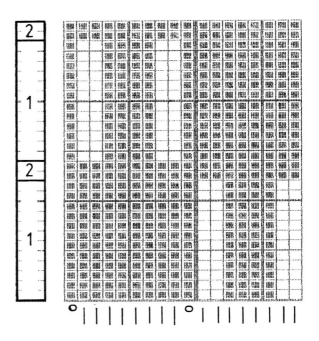

127 Patterncard with colour change and needle arrangement for figure 126

Knitting instructions for 126b
1 Cast on the required number of stitches
2 Set the machine and carriage as appropriate
3 Knit in slip stitch throughout changing the yarn as indicated

Exploring the bubble slip stitch patterncard

The bubble slip stitch patterncard can be altered in two ways.

1 By leaving needles out of work. Leave out of work each needle which lies between the slip stitch blocks (figure 126a).

2 By introducing colour. Introduce colour on the two stocking stitch rows between each row of bubbles. The colour outlines the shape and emphasizes it (figure 126b). The patterncard in figure 127 indicates where the empty needles and the colour change occur.

Tuck stitch variations

Many of the basic patterncards can be altered to produce interesting fabrics. In chapter 4 they have been altered by introducing extra stocking stitch rows. If these extra rows are knitted in a fine yarn and the pattern rows are knitted in a 4-ply yarn then the effect is most attractive (figure 128). Combining different yarn thicknesses is a very simple way of extending the potential of the basic patterncards.

124 Braids and edgings

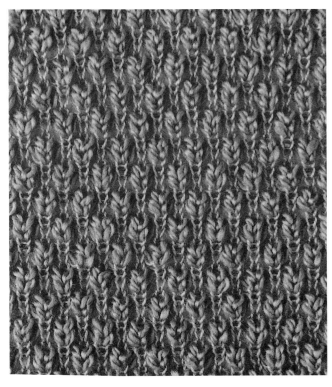

128 Mock blackberry stitch

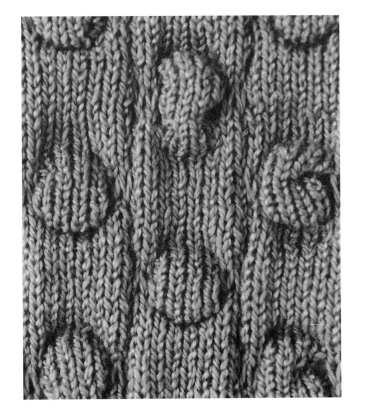

126a With needles out of work

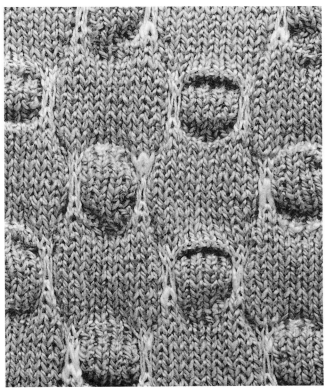

126b With a colour change

Developing the textured cable

Introducing fine yarn to the basic tuck alters the fabric quite considerably. If a fine yarn is introduced to the textured cables from chapter 4, the fine yarn moves to the knitside of the fabric and spreads out to form an oval shape (figure 129). The oval shape is obscured by the outer cable. If the outer curve is removed the textured centre is isolated creating a cable which looks as if it has been carved out of the fabric (figure 130).

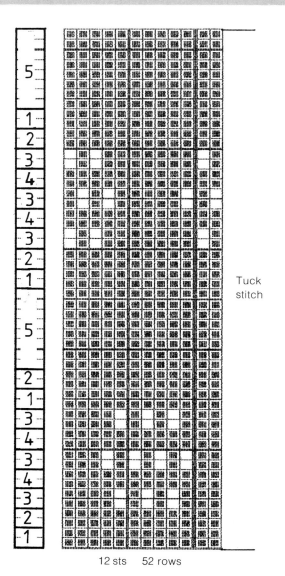

Tuck stitch

12 sts   52 rows

130b Patterncard

Yarn type

Colour 1 Background yarn plus lycra
Colour 2 Fine yarn – 2/30's cotton or bright acrylic
Colour 3 4-ply contrast yarn
Colour 4 Fine yarn plus lycra
Colour 5 4-ply background yarn

Knitting instructions

1 Cast on the required number of stitches
2 Set the machine and carriage as appropriate
3 Knit in tuck stitch throughout changing the yarn as indicated

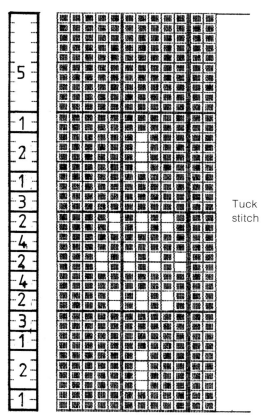

Tuck stitch

12 sts   40 rows

129b Patterncard

Yarn type

Colour 1 Background yarn plus lycra
Colour 2 4-ply contrast yarn
Colour 3 Fine yarn – 2/30's cotton or bright acrylic
Colour 4 Fine yarn plus lycra
Colour 5 4-ply background yarn

Knitting instructions

1 Cast on the required number of stitches
2 Set the machine and carriage as appropriate
3 Knit in tuck stitch throughout changing the yarn as indicated

129a Knitted sample

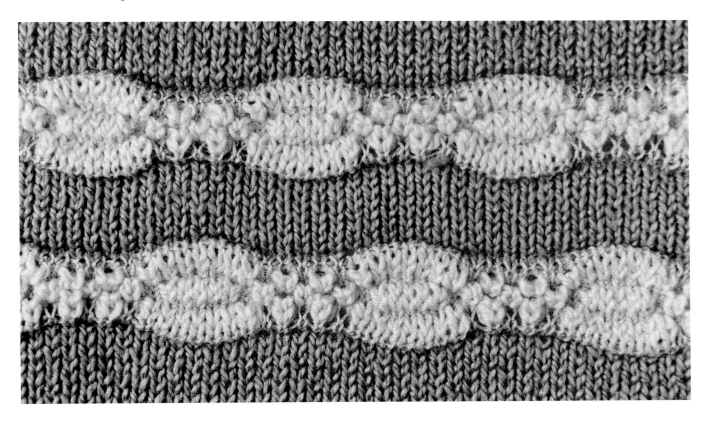

130a Perfected cables

The diagrams of these textured cables reveal how similar they are to the alternating diamond patterns in chapter 4 which were not totally successful. Unsightly ruching, shown in figure 42, was given as a reason for rejecting the patterncard. Closer inspection of the fabric revealed a ridged effect in the excess fabric which could be developed. The technique is an extension of the textured cables. The patterncard must be adapted to accommodate the extra stocking stitch rows to allow for the introduction of different yarns (figure 131a). A most unusual fabric results (figure 131b). Altering the type of yarn changes the emphasis of the design (figure 132).

The extension of the patterncard for owners of punchcard machines entails a lot of punching. To check whether the effect is worth the effort try locking the card at the end of each tucking sequence.

1 Release the tuck setting and change the yarn. Knit 1 row.

2 Reconnect the card to the patterning system. Knit 1 row.

3 Reset the carriage to tuck, change to main yarn, release the card and continue knitting.

Repeat steps 1 to 3 for the length of the punchcard.

Extending the patterncard for electronic owners is not as tedious. If the slip blocks are marked the adaptation is easier. Owners of the PPD will find manipulating the pattern is much easier with this type of marking. When the alteration is completed knit with the negative button in operation or use the variation switch on the PPD help menu.

There are many ways to develop this type of fabric.

1 Use the thick yarn for the tuck stitch rows and alter the sequence and type of yarn used for the stocking stitch rows.

2 Reduce the size of the diamonds in the patterncard in figure 42.

3 Change the shape of the tuck sections.

4 Use different thicknesses of yarn.

Tuck stitch

12 sts   62 rows

131b Patterncard

Yarn type
Colour 1 Fine yarn – 2/30's cotton or bright acrylic
Colour 2 4 ply contrast yarn
Colour 3 Fine yarn plus lycra
Colour 4 4 ply background yarn

Knitting instructions
1 Cast on the required number of stitches
2 Set the machine and carriage as appropriate
3 Knit in tuck stitch throughout changing the yarn as indicated

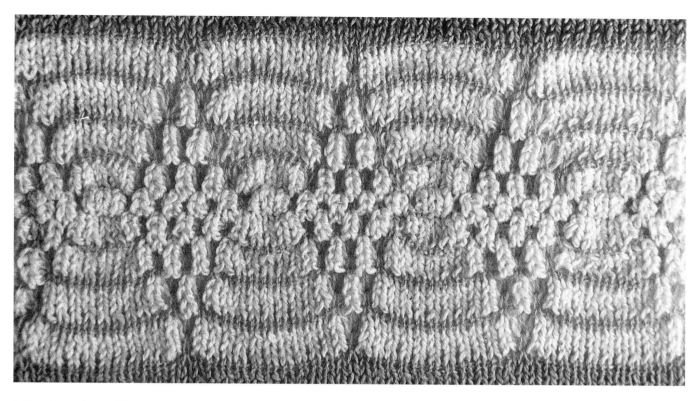

131a Extended cable

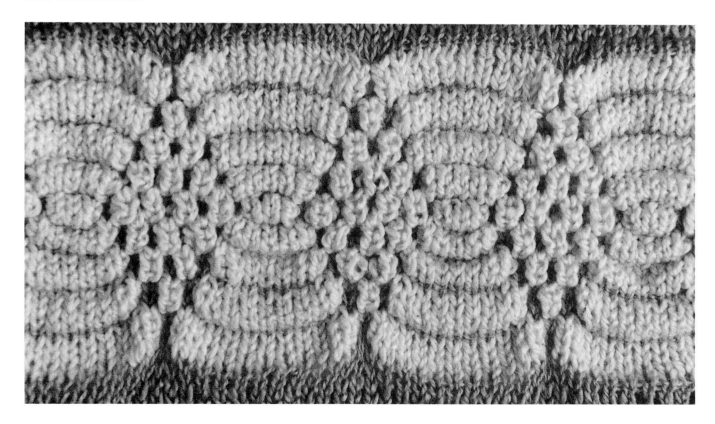

132a Extended cable with altered yarn change sequence

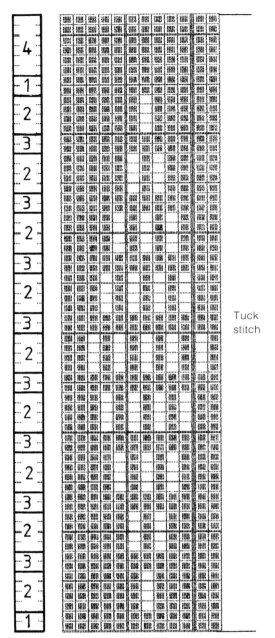

4
1
2
3
2
3
2
3
2
3
2
3
2
3
2
3
2
3
2
3
2
3
2
3
2
1

Tuck
stitch

12 sts   62 rows

132b Patterncard

Yarn type
As for figure 131

Knitting instructions
As for 131 with altered yarn change sequence

Tuck and slip combinations

Petal slip stitch can be combined with the tuck stitch cables from chapter 4 to create another version of the textured cables (figure 133).

In the original design a curve was created in the pattern by alternating blocks of tuck stitch and stocking stitch (figure 47). The tuck blocks on the patterncard draw in the fabric. The punched areas of the patterncard spread out the fabric. By placing a small slip stitch flower between the mock cables these features are further emphasized. The flower needs to be placed in the centre of the cable to create a more obvious curve. Petal slip stitch distorts fabric in a much more definite way than tuck stitch because, when knitted, the blank areas of the patterncard disappear behind the slip bars, the strands of knitting thus formed are only joined to the fabric at each side of the slipped sections.

When tuck stitch cards are knitted the blank areas of the card disappear but the strands of yarn which are formed are held in the needle hook until released by the patterncard. The loops thus formed are incorporated into the fabric which reduces the distortion.

Guidelines to designing textured mock cables

1 The shape of the outside cable is determined by the placing of the pattern sections.

2 The stitch used for the middle sections determines the depth of the curve.

This whole group of fabrics, developed from the original mittens, relies solely on the correct yarn change and the perception of an unknown individual to introduce lycra to patterned knitting rather than confine it to keeping welts in shape. The idea of introducing a fine yarn to outline the shapes requires the knowledge that a fine yarn always moves to the knitside of a fabric, and illustrates the importance of experimenting with altering the colour and/or the thickness of yarn.

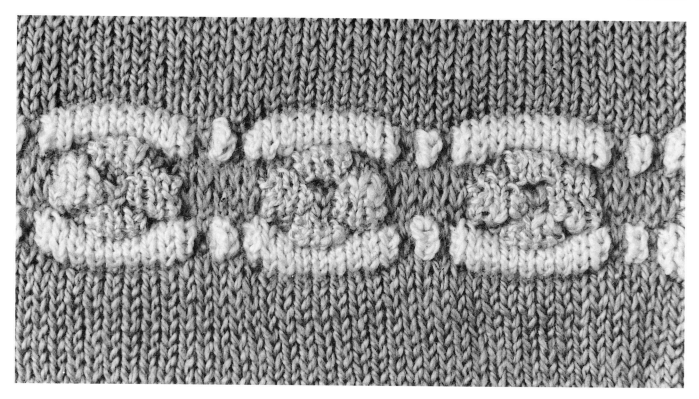

133a Cable with petal slip stitch

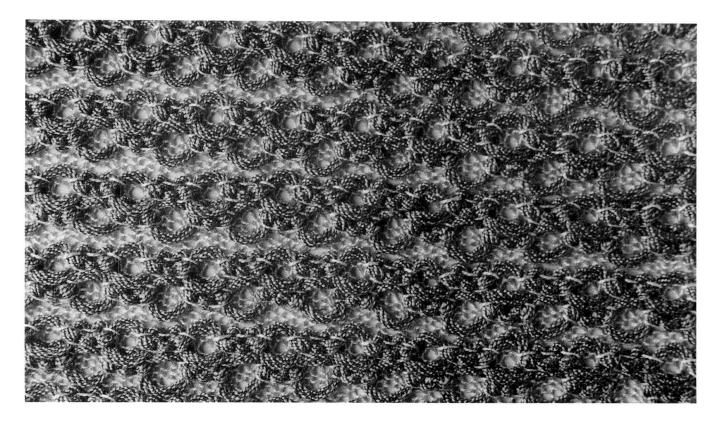

134a Slip and tuck

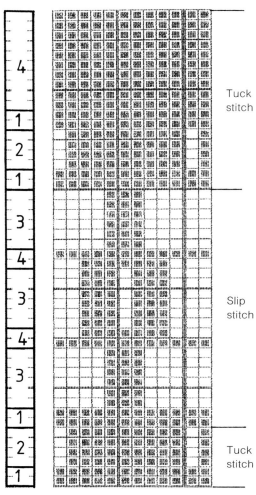

12 sts   48 rows

133b Patterncard

Yarn type
Colour 1 Main yarn plus lycra
Colour 2 Cable yarn same thickness as main yarn
Colour 3 Petal yarn slightly thinner than the
background yarn
Colour 4 Main yarn – any thickness up to 4 ply

Knitting instructions
1 Cast on the required number of stitches
2 Set the machine and carriage as appropriate
3 Knit for the required length changing the yarn and
the cam setting as indicated

Lace effects using tuck stitch and slip stitch combined

The extended basic cards with the extra rows
between each marked section can be further
extended to produce many interesting effects
using thick and thin yarn. The technique requires
that the difference between the yarn thicknesses
is extreme, e.g. two ends of 4-ply yarn and one
end of 2/30's yarn. This difference causes a
reaction when the fabric is released from the
machine. The fine yarn is stretched across the
needlebed until its release. It then contracts to its
natural size forcing the thick yarn to curve up or
down depending on the stitch setting in use
(figure 134).

Tuck and slip stitch are used on the alternate
patterning rows. The property of each stitch has
been studied. One aspect of each setting is
particularly important to the development of
different fabrics.

Tuck stitch loops are held in the hook of the
needle and remain at the top of the stitch when
released by the patterncard.

Slip stitch bars rest at the bottom of the stitch
and remain there when released.

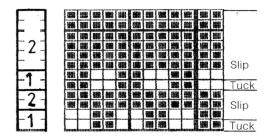

134b Patterncard

Yarn type
Colour 1 2/30's cotton or bright acrylic
Colour 2 two ends of 4 ply acrylic crepe

Knitting instructions
1 Cast on the required number of stitches
2 Set the machine and carriage as appropriate
3 Knit for the required length changing the yarn and
the cam setting as indicated

Knitting method

1 The patterning rows are knitted in the thick yarn.

2 The plain rows are knitted in the fine yarn.

3 One row of tuck stitch and one row of slip stitch is knitted on the pattern rows.

4 The plain rows are knitted in stocking stitch but because the patterncard is fully marked there is no need for a cam change.

5 Brother machines can knit tuck and slip on alternate rows automatically.

6 Knitmaster machines need to have a cam change after each patterning row.

There are many more ways of using the patterncards which have been created. Some may need to be altered; others may simply need a different yarn change sequence. The machine can be set in various ways to alter the pattern which will be produced. It is only by exploring these possibilities that machine knitting has developed to its present level of excellence. Learning the technique of patterncard design, understanding the patterncard and the machine should help machine knitters to extend the art even further.

YARN SUPPLIERS

UK

Bedford Sewing and Knitting Machines Ltd
13 Lime Street
Bedford, MK40 1LD
Machines, accessories, yarn, books and magazines

Jamieson and Smith Ltd
90 North Road
Lerwick
Shetland Isle, ZE1 0PQ
Shetland yarn only

Metropolitan
The Pinfold
Poole, Nantwich
Cheshire, CW5 6AL
Machines, accessories, yarn, books and magazines

Texere Yarns
College Mill
Barkerend Road
Bradford, BD3 9AQ
Yarns both natural and man-made

Worth Knitting
Silvercrest House
Wesley Road
Armley
Leeds, West Yorkshire
Machines, accessories, yarn, books and magazines

Yeoman Yarns Ltd
31 Leicester Road
Kibworth, Leicestershire
LE8 0NP

USA

Betty's Knit Shop
4020 Lambert Road
El Sobrante
CA 94803

Fiber Works
313 East 45th Street
New York 10017

Frances Collins
Importer (Bramwell Yarns)
PO Box 8244
Midland, TX 79708

The Knitting Machine Centre
5443 Cannas Drive
Cincinatti
Ohio 45238

AUSTRALIA

Bendigo Woollen Mills
PO Box 119
Kangaroo Flat
Victoria 3555, Australia

Regent Knitwear
138–140 Regent Street
Redfern 2016

'Tessa B' Knits
98A Norma Road
Myaree 6154
Western Australia

Taxtor Trading Co
9 Brighton Street
Richmond 3121
Australia

SUNDRIES

R L & C M Bond
Town Street
Farsley, Pudsey
West Yorkshire
Beads, braids, buttons, sewing thread, sequins, beaded motifs, etc

The Textile Bookshop
Tynwald Mills
St John's
Isle of Man
Proportional graph paper available by mail order; callers by appointment only

Densafilm and other types of plastic carbon are available from most good stationers.

BOOK LIST

Kate Armitage
Card 3, MSM Publications,
Bournemouth 1985

Tuck knitting designs and patterns, Regine Faust,
published by
Regine Studio, Knit Designs,
Toronto, Ontario

To and Fro Postal Knitting Club
PO Box 172
Maidenhead
Berkshire SL6 8XH
Published quarterly

Kathleen Kinder
The Machine Knitters Book of the Ribber, Vols 1 and 2,
Kathleen Kinder, Settle 1984 and 1985

Mosaic Floatless Fair Isle,
Kathleen Kinder, Settle 1987

Techniques of Machine Knitting, Batsford, London
1983

Machine Knitting: The Technique of Knitweave,
Batsford, London 1987

Machine Knitting: The Technique of Lace, Batsford,
London 1991

The Art of Motif Knitting and Twenty Four Stitch Design,
Kathleen Kinder, Settle 1988

Suzanna Lewis
The Machine Knitters Guide to Creating Fabrics, Lark Books
1986

Sheila McGregor
The Complete Book of Fair Isle Knitting, Batsford, London
1981

Denise Musk
Machine Knitting: The Technique of Slipstitch,
Batsford, London, 1989

Barbara Walker
A Treasury of Knitting Patterns, Scribners and Sons,
New York 1968

A Second Treasury of Knitting Patterns, Scribners, New York
1970

Charted Knitting Designs, A Third Treasury of Knitting Patterns, Scribners and Sons,
New York 1972

Mary Weaver
The Ribbing Attachment Part
1, Weaverknits Ltd
(Publications) 1974

The Ribbing Attachment Part
2, Weaverknits Ltd
(Publications) 1976

Machine Knitting News
published by
Litharne Ltd, PO Box 9
Stratford-upon-Avon
Warwickshire, CV37 8 RS

INDEX